Bridge is my game

Lessons of a Lifetime

Bridge is my game

Lessons of a Lifetime

by Chas H Goren

with Jack Olsen

Cornerstone Library
Published by Simon & Schuster
New York

Copyright © 1965 by Chancellor Hall Ltd.

Published by Cornerstone Library
A Simon & Schuster Division of
Gulf & Western Corporation
Simon & Schuster Building
1230 Avenue of the Americas
New York, New York 10020
CORNERSTONE LIBRARY and colophon are
trademarks of Simon & Schuster, registered in
the U.S. Patent and Trademark Office.

This new Cornerstone Library edition is published by
arrangement with Doubleday & Company, Inc. and is a
complete and unabridged reprint of the original hardcover
edition.

Manufactured in the United States of America

10 9 8 7 6 5

ISBN 0-346-12306-2

CONTENTS

1   *Free yourself of fads and gimmicks*   9

Advice to a young bridge player   10
"Tell me, do you play bridge?"   12
Know Thyself   14
Virtuosity goes unrewarded   16
There are four sides to a bridge table   18
Always, there's the exception   22

2   *A plan for bolder, better bidding*   25

How to be a swashbuckler   26
The winning way is the simple way   28
The hand only you can play   29
The use — and dangers — of the short-club
      convention   31

3   *Successful communication*   35

When modesty is the best policy   36
Are you giving away your secrets?   38
"I told you not to look at your hand."   41
Who should play the slam?   42

4   *Getting the best result* possible   45

What to do with an immoderate partner   46
The right bid . . . but the wrong partner   48
Bridge, too, has its bullies   50
My first, unforgettable game with Ely Culbertson   53

Contents

5   *The double: triumph, fun
. . . and trouble*   57

If you cannot double, you cannot win   58
When *not* to double   59
The special situation of the powerhouse double   60
Strange holdings and how to spot them   64
The beauty of the probing double   67

6   *Doubling as offensive strategy*   73

How to handle an overcaller   74
The odds will be in your favor   76
Slam doubles and the victimized doubler   82
The other side of the coin   85

7   *The obstacle course of conventions*   91

"Explain 'em to yourselves!"   92
Are we speaking the same language?   93
Some classic lapses of communication   95
The less you assume, the further ahead you'll be   97
The Goren system revealed   99
The one no-trump opening: can it ever fail?   101
Aren't we forgetting something?   102

8   *Tricks of my trade*   105

Play the cards, not the rules   106
A lesson in deception   108
Finesses I have known   112
My short cut to the count   115
The subtle art of playing blind   118

9   *Table tactics of a game for four*   125

Bridge is one part psychology   126
You can find profit in a poor partnership   128
A special kind of demon: the tyrant   130

Three rules of the road   134
When everything depends on the anonymity of
your hand   136
The case of the missing card   138
He who hesitates . . .   140
The rapid-fire man   142

10   *Reflections on a lifetime*   145

The Quizzes   153

Quiz 1   155
Quiz 2   160
Quiz 3   165
Quiz 4   171
Quiz 5   176
Quiz 6   181
Quiz 7   186

Free yourself
  of fads and gimmicks

When I was studying law at McGill University, a girl taught me how to play bridge. "Just follow suit," she said. "If you can't, you discard or you trump." So I followed suit, and when I couldn't, I discarded or I trumped. At the end of the afternoon, I was down about 4000 points and that lovely, intelligent, desirable girl was laughing at me.

You might suppose that I now look back in anger at my first bridge teacher. Well, no, I don't. In the first place, she had made me so ashamed that I went home that summer and practically memorized a book on bridge, thus inadvertently taking the first step toward a life you might describe as all play and no work. And looking backward, I now realize that her simple instructions to me were the essence of what one *should* tell a beginner. *Just follow suit. If you can't, you discard or you trump.* You cannot expect a first-timer to assimilate much more than that, at least for a few rubbers.

But consider the same situation as it might happen today. A mythical Charles Goren, McGill class of '65, wants to learn bridge.

"Well, Charlie," his beautiful (I'm making up this situation, and I say she's beautiful) girl friend tells him, "it's simple. First let's talk about bidding. Suppose your partner opens the bidding with one club."

"That means he has a lot of clubs in his hand, right?" interrupts the precocious young man.

"No, not exactly. Maybe he's playing the Neapolitan Club—"

"Which means?"

"—That he has at least 17 points in high cards, but not necessarily any good clubs."

"Well, *that's* confusing," says young Goren. "And anyway, why would anybody want to reach all the way to

Naples for a system? Wouldn't they be more likely to use some American system like the—"

"The Vanderbilt Club?" she interrupts. "Well, if you are playing the Vanderbilt Club, an opening bid of one club can mean you hold more than half the high cards in the deck."

"And good clubs, of course?"

"No, it doesn't mean a thing about clubs."

"Now I'm beginning to catch on," he cries. "If my partner opens a club, it has nothing to do with clubs. It just means he has a good hand."

"Yes and no," she says, a touch of irritation crossing her lovely face. "An opening bid of one club can also mean that your hand is just average but you've got a real good club suit. So you open a club."

The fellow we've been picturing now ponders, frets, puzzles and wonders. Finally he announces: "I've got it! Yes, it's all clear to me—if you have good clubs, you open one club. But if you don't have good clubs, you open one club."

"Don't get smart with me!"

"But that's exactly what you said!"

The smoke clears, peace is waged, and poor Goren is slowly taught the Roman Club, the Neapolitan Club, the Vanderbilt Club, the Schenken Club, the Roth-Stone Club, the Kaplan-Sheinwold Club, and the Standard American Club, at which point he explains to his friend that he feels he has mastered the various meanings of a one-club opening bid.

"What do you mean, you've mastered them!" she snorts. "There are thirty-seven more!"

The mythical Charles Goren, McGill '65, flings the deck into the air and stalks off into the night, destined—alas!—to go through life as a professional player of Milles Bornes. He will never understand Milles Bornes either, but at least that card game doesn't have any clubs to figure out.

"Tell me, do you play bridge?"

If you get the impression from this little flight of fancy that I do not approve of all the artificial, meaningless, useless embroidery that is slowly covering up the rich tapestry of contract bridge, you are absolutely right. Woodrow Wilson talked about "open covenants openly arrived at" fifty years ago, but the phrase remains the best description of accurate, informative bidding. Not only is clear, natural bidding best for the dunderheads, which is a minor argument on its behalf, but it is also best for the most brilliant players on earth. And I firmly believe that if I had been confronted with some of today's bidding systems when I first sat down at a bridge table—more years ago than it is decent to divulge—I would never have learned the game. It simply would have been more trouble than it would have been worth. Which brings us to the most important point about modern contract bridge. It may seem naive but I'll run the risk of offending you and make the point anyway:

Bridge is for fun

You should play the game for no other reason. You should not play bridge to make money, to show how smart you are, to show how stupid your partner is, to prove that you are the greatest teacher since Socrates, to show off the latest fad in bidding, or to prove any of the several hundred other things that bridge players are so often trying to prove. The instant you find yourself playing bridge for an object other than the enjoyment the game offers, you should rack it up and go on to something else—court tennis maybe, or Old Maid. Anything but bridge.

If, on the other hand, you *are* having fun, then be advised that the sharper your game becomes the stiffer the competition, the more skilled and intelligent the company, the more fun you'll have. First, however, you'd better stop and check and make sure that you're playing bridge, *contract bridge*, the game as invented, more or less, by Harold

Vanderbilt some thirty-five years ago. I was reminded of all this a while back. I was in an anteroom waiting to be interviewed by a radio announcer, something I have experienced perhaps a thousand times in my life. The interviewer came in and said, "Okay, Mr. Goren, let's rehearse."

"Rehearse?" I said. "Can't we just go on cold? You ask the questions and I'll answer them."

"No, sir," he said. "I find it's best to rehearse first."

So we began the rehearsal. The announcer introduced himself, cleared his throat, introduced me as Charles Goren of Miami Beach, Florida, cleared his throat again, and released his first question in pear-shaped tones:

"Tell me, Mr. Goren, do you play bridge?"

The question amused me for several weeks, until I realized that it was not so ridiculous after all. One night I was kibitzing a big local tournament and after watching play for a couple of hours, I realized that three quarters of the people there were *not* playing contract bridge. Oh, they thought they were. They knew how to count points. They knew how many it takes to open, to respond, to jump, to jump-shift; they knew how many points made game in a major, game in a minor, slam and grand slam. But for the most part they were not there to play bridge. Or, to put it another way: they were playing bridge, but playing bridge was not the real reason they were there. Some of them had fallen for one of the new gimmick systems and were spending the evening baffling opponents and partners alike with bids that nobody understood and which, if understood, would not have been wise bids anyway. That is not bridge; it is mnemonics. Others were following all the old chestnut rules: cover an honor with an honor, second hand low, third hand high, never finesse your partner, and a good cigar is a smoke. That is not bridge; it is slavery. Then there were the usual tyrannical players blowing their tops at partners who had failed to return their leads. That is not bridge; it is sadism. And their partners would sit patiently and take all this abuse. That is not bridge; it is masochism.

Know thyself

Of all the failings I noticed, the most common was a childlike faith in points and the point count system. What's that you are asking? You are asking if it could be possible that after all these years of drumming the point count system into our heads, he's now going to tell us to forget it? Not in the least. But I *am* going to suggest that you supplement point count with some good old common sense. I've been saying *that* for years, too, but apparently not everybody has been listening. Too many players are lazily counting their hands and then letting what they consider the point count system dictate their bids. But one thing it does not specify: it does not insist that you abandon all the workings of your cerebral cortex and your medulla oblongata, not to mention your eyes and your ears.

The paradoxical fact about bridge as it is being played these days is that many players are ruining their games by trying far too much far too soon. Suppose I told you that you could simplify your game immeasurably, and *at the same time improve it immeasurably*. Suppose I told you that the more bridge complexities, subtleties, and nuances you try to cram into your game, the worse your game is going to be. Suppose I had the colossal gall to charge you with spending too much of your bridge energy trying to perfect superduper devices that are not worth learning, and at the same time failing to learn basic techniques that make the difference between winners and losers. Suppose I told you all that. Would you be insulted? Would you read on?

Okay, now that we're rid of the hotheads, let's be more specific. Here are the basic faults you and I are going to uncover in the average American bridge player:

- ♣ He gives away thousands of points a year with stereotyped, predictable bidding and play.

- ♦ He often doubles when he shouldn't and more often fails to double when he should.

♥ He rigidly obeys rules that are nothing more than general guidelines intended for the rankest of beginners.

♠ He engages in repetitious mannerisms, right down to such minor matters as the way he sorts his cards, thereby giving valuable information to experienced opponents.

♣ He persists in attempting plays he doesn't understand, and the same time failing to try plays he does understand (and which have just as good a mathematical chance of success).

♦ He treats his partner like a lackey, or allows his partner to treat him like one, in either case destroying the calm, warm rapport that spells points to any team on any level.

♥ He considers only his own hand and tries to turn bridge into a singles event.

♠ And there are many others.

The starting point for correcting these deficiencies is the advice of that great contract bridge teacher, Solon. Whereas most players think that better bridge means learning more and more conventions and more and more razzle-dazzle plays, better bridge really begins with Know Thyself. It is exactly the same as golf. I may have a perfect lie for a four wood, but the four wood is a club that history has shown clearly I can't handle. So I put it away regretfully and use a three iron and wind up twenty yards short of the green. But I'm not disturbed. With the four wood, I'd have wound up twenty yards *past* the green— the *other* green. By Knowing Myself on the golf course, knowing what clubs I can handle and what clubs I can't, I will wind up with a six on this hole, which is better than my average.

Now take yourself at the bridge table. You are playing a contract that has a fifty-fifty chance of making with a finesse. But another possible approach comes to your mind: a double squeeze with a dummy reversal. Which approach do you try? If you understand finessing better than you understand double-squeeze-with-a-dummy-reversal-ing, stick with the fifty-fifty, and you'll come out far ahead in the long pull. Fight down the urge to try the gaudy, fancy play until you have a better idea what you are doing.

Virtuosity goes unrewarded

In addition to understanding your own bridge game, your own strengths and weaknesses, you must try to figure out your partner's game. Is he an overbidder or an underbidder? Can he read signals? If so, *what* signals? There's no point in giving him a signal he doesn't understand. The opponents might understand and become the only ones to profit. And therein lies another fundamental of bridge:

> Play your partner's game, especially if you
> know more about bridge than he does.

In certain types of games, notably rubber bridge and money bridge, knowing more than your partner does can hurt you badly. I have had an inordinate amount of good fortune in individual events in which one is faced with a strange partner every time he turns around. There it soon becomes a case of adapt-or-perish. One reason for my happy record in individual play is an ability to sense very quickly the weaknesses and deficiencies in my new partner's game. Many times there were superior bids available to me, bids which would have stood them on their ears in the Saturday night game at the Regency Club. But more often than not I would refrain from such big-league bids because I knew my partners wouldn't grasp them. I won the Chicago *Tribune*'s individual tournament three years out of five (the normal expectancy would be to win it about one year out of forty) not because of the outstanding bids and plays I made but because of the ones I declined to make. All around me were the hotshots of bridge, making dazzling false cue bids, Texas transfers, and South African slip-under leads, and across from them were sitting strange partners whose faces were the perfect personification of a single word: *"Huh?"*

The fact is that stripping your game back to essentials can produce winning bridge in any circles, not just in cut-around rubber games or open-to-the-public individual events. Your mind simply doesn't have to be awhirl with Italian openings and short clubs and anti-no-trump conventions and weak two bids and all the other equipment of the collector of conventions. Most of my teaching has been based on the premise that an uncluttered game is the most effective. I've played with more partners than anybody in the history of bridge: on footlockers in baseball dressing rooms, on airplanes crossing both oceans, in the salons of Europe and the one-room walk-ups of South Philadelphia, in stuffy auditoriums on floodlit stages and in television studios, and I have found that any partner could understand my game and with hardly any exceptions I could understand his. Once somebody called me the "Simple Simon" of bridge. I said, "Thank you. I appreciate the compliment."

The Complex Simons of bridge, the players who rush from convention to convention and system to system, give me a pain, not merely because they are slowing down their own progress toward genuine bridge skill, but because they make life so unpleasant for everybody else. The player who arrives at a tournament with a long list of artificial conventions is spending too much time trying to win instead of trying to have fun. The irony is he'll wind up doing neither. This sort of a player is a burden to himself, his partners, and his opponents. He is like the pseudo-sophisticate who sits down to his first Chinese meal and insists on using chopsticks. If somebody doesn't set him straight, he is going to starve midway between the shark's-fin soup and the egg rolls.

At the other end of the spectrum, of course, we have the terrified player who thinks that simplicity means obeying a certain set of rules and never deviating from them. I can bear this sort of partner provided that   *a*] I find out about him before too much harm is done to our partnership, and   *b*] he keeps quiet when *I* violate one of *his* sacred tenets. But I must admit to seeing more than one shade of red when, after the opposition makes a tough contract, one of these players says to me: "Well, after all, partner, you *did* lead low from a king doubleton! After that there was no way to set them." This is a character we've all met, unfortunately, the player who must follow the old bromides to the letter because there is nothing between his ears to take their place. He plays bridge by rote. I usually can contain myself, but what I really want to do is spear him with a cruel stare and then state in a totally calm way: "I know your rules, partner . . . I used to follow them myself, in the first three days I played bridge. I know you never lead low from a doubleton king. And I know you never lead a king from a doubleton king. Those are wonderful rules, and *you* are wise to follow them. But there are some contracts that can only be set by underleading the king doubleton. And there are others that can only be set by a lead of the king from king-small. In fact, partner, I would classify those leads as two basic tools on defense. I would explain these situations to you, but you probably wouldn't approve." And he wouldn't. Or else he wouldn't be playing Old Maxim Bridge.

There are four sides to a bridge table

Annoying as the rote player may be, he is topped by the man who plays *his* hand, his *whole* hand and nothing *but* his hand. He is not the least concerned by the fact that he has a partner and the partner is also holding thirteen cards. This fellow may refuse to open with 14 points ("I didn't like the looks of them, partner"), or he may open a hand with 10 points ("I really didn't have a bid, but that spade suit looked so good"). As his unfortunate partner, you will open one heart with a hand counting 21 points, intending to jump on the next round, but there won't be a next round because Old Bullhead over there, holding seven points, will pass ("it didn't look like we had any kind of fit").

Or if he has a long suit, he will bid it all night before letting you have the contract in your own longer, stronger suit. He reckons that six solid hearts in his own hand are far better than eight solid spades in the partnership, especially when one considers that he will be playing the hearts and everybody knows that is worth two tricks right there. So he goes down three in his suit where a game in your suit was a laydown. Only once have I ever seen such a partner subdued, and it took a little bold coffeehousing to do it. The bidding went:

South (our stubborn friend): One heart.
North: One spade.
South: Two hearts.
North: Two spades.
South: Three hearts.
North: Three spades!
South: Four hearts.
North: I bid the fourth and last spade!

I have painted this type of player in loud colors, and probably you don't recognize anything about him in yourself. But there is a bit of stubbornness in all of us; we all tend to play and bid our thirteen cards as if they were the entire deck. Take a typical situation. How would you react if you picked up the following hand.

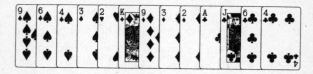

Well, it's not the Mona Lisa, is it? It counts 10 points on the surface of it, but on the other hand 11 of its 13 cards appear to be sure losers. Despite its 10 points, the hand is only 1½ tricks better than a Yarborough * and many a

* A hand that holds no face cards.

player would sort the cards, yawn gapingly and say, "C'mon, c'mon, whose bid is it?" showing everybody at the table that this is one hand he'd like to get over quickly.

But if you'll take another look at that hand you'll see that there is absolutely no way to evaluate it until your partner has had a chance to bid. If he bids *anything*, this handful of nothing suddenly begins to look decent. If partner bids one spade, the hand looks downright strong. And if he opens with a two demand, you're holding a power-house.

As it turned out when this hand was held in the South position during a tournament, the bidding began as follows:

East	South	West	North
1 ♥	Pass	2 ♥	Dbl
Pass	?		

At this point, South had to make a complete re-evaluation of the hand he had been feeling so gloomy about. Off the bidding, it had now become clear that East and West had a pile of hearts and apparently little else. South's one heart, therefore, was money in the bank; it promised only a single heart loser, no matter how many hearts the enemy had. South's next problem was to figure out what his partner was holding. At this stage of the bidding, he marked North for 16 points. The logic was simple: a double of one shows at least the equivalent of an opening bid, or about 13 points; therefore North's double of two should be at least one trick better than an opening bid, or about 16 points. Now South could begin to add points: 16 in the North hand and 10 in his own. It seemed to add up to game and left South with but two problems: how to show North that his hand was better than it had sounded so far in the bidding, and how to find out North's best suit. Take another look at South's hand and see if you can figure out his bid.

His bid was three hearts, and if you figured it correctly, you are an exceedingly rare bridge player. That bid of three hearts is right out of the big time. North took it as strength, and showed his spades; South raised to game, and the contract was made easily. Here are the four hands:

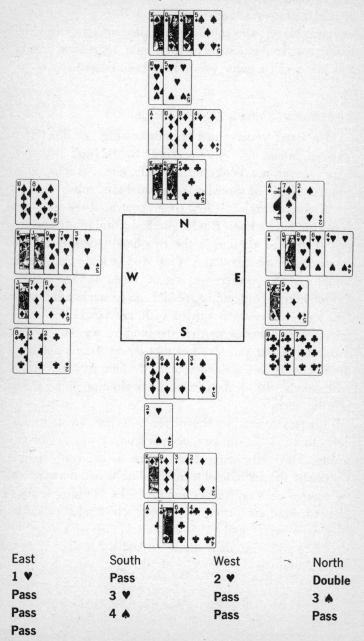

East	South	West	North
1 ♥	Pass	2 ♥	Double
Pass	3 ♥	Pass	3 ♠
Pass	4 ♠	Pass	Pass
Pass			

The lessons in this hand are many and varied. South's unpromising cards turned out to be the balance of power even in the face of the adverse bidding. But had South been a typical player who could not see past his own cards, he would not have looked favorably upon aggressive action, and as a result a game would have been missed.

Always, there's the exception

The hand we have just been discussing also illustrates why one cannot always go precisely by the book – whether it be one of my books or anybody else's. Technically, South's cue bid of three hearts violated the "rules." Such a bid is supposed to show first-round control of the suit, and South did have a loser. But he also had a brain; he could see that there was a game in the two hands, despite all the frantic bidding by East and West. And he knew that North would never know there was a game unless the South hand did something bold and aggressive. So he made a false cue bid, and virtue was rewarded with 120 points below the line. You say you agree that the bidding was strong and imaginative, but you also feel that it was dangerous? Ah, but it was not half so dangerous, in the long run, as treating such hands with disdain from the beginning, and quickly passing them out.

I hope that this has shown you that there are no bridge rules that can't be broken, no bad hands that can't be upgraded into better hands, no situation that can't be improved by the addition of a little old-fashioned horse sense, no 100 per cent valid DO's and DON'Ts. Nothing is absolute in bridge, except certain partners who remind me of the man who said: "Only a fool is certain about things."

"Are you sure about that?" asked a friend.

"Absolutely."

One sad fact of bridge is that there *have* to be losers, and I'm afraid there is absolutely nothing you and I can do about them. There are always going to be millions of bridge players who will never make an end play, an uppercut, or a squeeze in their lives, except accidentally; there are millions who, after the second lead, won't have the foggiest idea what cards have dropped; millions whose biggest achievement is that once in a while, when it really matters, they will count trump right down to the last trick and only be one or two off in their count; millions whose slogan should be: "An opening bid facing an opening bid produces down one." What are we to do with them?

Nothing. Let them slumber. If it weren't for all those losers, what would we winners be? Losers: that's what we'd be. But come to think of it, I could never be a loser. It is, in fact, impossible, and all because of a tip given to me years ago by George S. Kaufman. It was George who pointed out that you could always hold good cards *merely by sitting South*. "No matter who writes the books or articles," he said, "South holds the most terrific cards that I ever saw. There is a lucky fellow if I ever saw one."

Ever since then, I have always sat South. That is the secret of my success, and I pass it along to you for whatever it is worth.

2

A plan for bolder,
better bidding

How to be a swashbuckler

Remember the Charles Atlas ads? "I was a 97-pound weakling." Happily, most of the 97-pound weaklings seem to have disappeared from the American scene. But they have not disappeared from the bridge table.

Don't ask me what it is about a deck of cards that can change a dynamic, forceful, intelligent person into a Caspar Milquetoast, underbidding and underplaying his hand, cringing and covering up, squirming under the gaze of partner and opponents alike. "That's not *me!*" you say? You're a regular Commando Kelly of the bridge table? Well, then you are the exception. Most of our so-called average players tend to play it on the safe—and nervous—side. They will count their points ten times during the bidding and come up with nine different answers. They will pass out hands that hold a sound possibility of game, hoping that the next deal will present them with something easier (like a blockbuster on which they can bid game and make slam). At the end of the evening, they will be down a couple of thousand points, and they will wend their miserable way home saying to each other, "Gee, how did we lose all that money? We were bidding quite conservatively."

Exactly.

To twist one of the great maxims of history into a basic maxim of bridge:

> Spineless bridge loses, and absolutely
> spineless bridge loses absolutely.

The logic behind this is complex, but it hangs mostly on the following fact: the mathematics of contract bridge is such that the timid bidder is punished far more severely for his timidity than the bold bidder is punished for his boldness. The timid bidder fails to make rubbers, rarely worth less than 700 to 1,000 points. The bold bidder gets set, costing 50 to 200 points, rarely more. By a ratio of about five to one, the game is rigged for the adventuresome, the bold and the brave. I know it doesn't look that way sometimes. There's a big 800 points on the score where Mr. Bold was set, and 800 seems to be too much to swap for anything less than an opponents' slam. But how much did Mr. Bold *actually* lose? Well, the game and rubber the opponents could have made were worth about 600, so Mr. Bold lost 200 points. Mr. Milquetoast's score shows no such oppressive disasters. But that doesn't mean they aren't there. In fact, they're bigger, even if they are invisible. Because when Mr. Milquetoast stopped at three spades and made four, he scored 90 points below the line and 30 above. If he had bid four, he'd have scored 120 below and 500 above. He lost 500 points right then and there. But he may have lost far more. If he had bid four spades, maybe the opponents would have gone out on a limb to save the game, taking an 800 point set. And sometimes, if Mr. Milquetoast bids four spades when he can't make it, he'll find his opponents taking a phantom save that will net him from 300 to 500 points. The fact is, you only have to make one doubtful game in three to come out with a profit. Notice I didn't say the mathematics of the game is rigged "for the reckless, the wild and the foolish." There's a difference. And if you will put yourself in my care for a while, I will try to show you the difference, and at the same time try to change your entire approach to the game. If you are a good student, it will not be long before you will *appear* to be the most swashbuckling bidder on the block. You will be doubling more than you ever did in the past, and you will even be *redoubling* now and then. (Tell the truth, now; when was the last time you redoubled? 1947? 1937? If you're the average player, you redouble about as often as you have your appendix out.) You will be bidding more slams and approaching them by a more direct route. On occasion, you are even going to throw the Goren system clean out the window in favor of your own personal judgment. In short, you are going to be hell on wheels.

And how is this grand transmutation to come about?

Not with any of bridge's miracle tonics, but with simple arithmetic, simple logic, simple bridge. We are going to revive some of the eternal verities that are slowly being drowned in the flood of snake oil. We are going to return to the wonderful purity and logic so well expressed by William Somerset Maugham when he said: "If you have a cool head, the ability to put two and two together and get the right answer, and if you will tell the exact truth about your hand, you will be a useful partner and a formidable opponent."

The winning way is the simple way

Let us start, for, simplicity's sake, by showing how a typically complex situation can be made simpler. The problem: how to tell if your hand is worth an opening bid of two in a suit? The "scientific" way is to count your points and open with a two demand if you have:

- 25 points and a good five-card suit.
- 23 points and a good six-card suit.
- 21 points and a good seven-card suit.

I devised that formula years ago after consultation with other players and a fine mathematician, William M. Anderson of Toronto. The formula is foolproof and if you use it for the rest of your life it will be impossible for you to go very far wrong on two-bids. However . . .

There is another way, and it is just about as foolproof as the above. Count your losing cards. *If you hold game minus one trick in your own hand*, open two. Using this device, you can forget all about the numbers. It is neither more nor less effective than the number system, but for many players it is easier to remember.

Or take another standard bid: the pre-emptive opening, sometimes called the barricade bid, a quick bid of three or four to show a weak hand but a long suit. The aim is to take away the opponents' bidding room, to force them to start their own bidding at a high level. The bid is defensive and is made in the full expectation that it can be doubled and set.

Altogether too many players are abusing this bid frightfully. They make it when they hold as many as 12 or 13 points, and if their partners turn out to be holding, the barricade bidders learn too late that it is their own partnerships they have barricaded. Or they will make the pre-emptive opening when they hold seven spades to the jack and not another face card, thus risking a huge set. All the numerical rules for pre-emptive openings are carefully set forth in approximately a hundred different books on bridge. Roughly, the bid requires a high-card holding of 10 points or less, vulnerable, or 9 or less, not vulnerable. But if you can't remember that, remember this: *If you can win seven tricks in your own hand but your hand is not good enough for a normal opening bid, make a pre-emptive opening.* It's as simple as that.

I have cited these two examples not with any hope that they will revolutionize your game, but merely to show you that almost all the complex numbers of bridge are based, after all, on simple axioms and simple truths. You can use the numbers or you can use the truth behind the numbers, whichever is easier for you, but whatever you use, make it your genie, not your master.

The hand only you can play

No matter how knowledgeable the elder statesmen like me may seem to you, remember that you have one big advantage over us. When we devised our systems, we were not looking at your hand. *You* are. And since your hand is one out of a possible 635,013,559,600 bridge hands, there may be something about it that cannot be handled by the numbers. For example:

It is a cornerstone of almost all modern bridge that a hand counting 14 points *must* be opened, and indeed it must. But compare this 14-point hand:

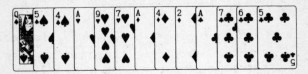

with this one:

Each hand counts 14 points, but is there anybody in the world who would argue that the second hand isn't clearly superior? Take another look at the first hand. Unless something happens to promote that queen, this hand is worth three tricks, leaving a mere ten tricks available to the opponents if partner comes up busted. But the second hand is a cinch for six tricks, regardless of partner's holdings, and if partner does have 10 or 11 points, the hand may easily make game.

If your tendency in the past has been to evaluate two such 14-point hands as about the same, you have been missing the point of the point count, which was invented *to assist your mental processes, not replace them*. To paraphrase the late George Orwell, all 14-point hands are equal, but some are more equal than others. Only you, looking at the hand, the score, the caliber of opposition, the capabilities of your partner, can make the final decision.

But this requires mental effort, doesn't it? Aye, there's the rub. All too many players nowadays (and let's hope this doesn't include you) would rather pick cotton than put out one erg of mental energy. They reason that the game wouldn't be as much fun if they had to think; so they fall back on systems and bromides. The paradoxical truth is they'd have far more fun and do much less work if they'd use their own heads now and then.

The use—and dangers—of the "short club convention"

The lazy players make up the breed which has brought the one-club opening, the so-called "short club," into wild and woolly vogue. The "short club convention" (I put it in quotes because among reliable players there is no such animal) is the favorite of the player who doesn't necessarily have good clubs but figures he can support anything else bid by partner. The response he often gets to the artificial one-club opening is two clubs, and another popular response is one no trump, each of which leaves the opener right back where he started—scratching around for a decent suit. Except that now he's scratching around at a higher level.

Before you accuse me of not having any imagination and verve, let me quickly point out that I am aware of a few circumstances under which an expert might open one club without holding a strictly biddable club suit. Suppose he came up with a hand like this:

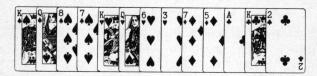

His hand is strong, but he has no overpoweringly attractive opening bid. If he can catch partner with a biddable major, there should be a shot at game. If he can find partner with good diamonds, there is probably a game at three no trump. A game in clubs is not entirely out of the question, if partner has four or five clubs and 9 or 10 points. So there is sanity to a one-club opening bid here, and no danger of getting chewed up badly.

But look how the bid is being used practically everywhere bridge is played. A lazy player will pick up:

And he will open one club. He figures it's too daring, too bold, and too much work to open that spade suit with the king missing. Let his partner select a suit, and our lazy opener will follow him to the end of the earth (and sometimes a little beyond) with vigorous support. The fact is that nothing is served by the club opener that cannot be served by a normal, natural opening of one spade. But suppose the contract is dropped at one club. This time the opener is going to get dumped for a fifteen-yard loss. I could understand his willingness to run this risk if there were some advantage to be derived from the one-club opening. But there is none.

Often you will hear such bidders ask if you play the "short-club convention." Should you cut such a person as partner in a strange game, there *is* one way to come out on top: feign serious illness and beat a hasty retreat. There is no such device as a "short-club convention," and until the establishment of bridge loses its collective marbles, there will be no such convention. And yet the "short-club" bid remains popular. Its practitioners have now become so enamored of their passive bid that I saw one of them open a club recently with this holding:

Admittedly, he had a problem with those two shaky majors. But if he had to make an artificial bid in the hope of finding his partner with a major suit fit, why in the world didn't he bid one diamond? It has the same effect as the club opening and offers far less possibility of disaster. I asked this gentleman about his bid later that evening.

"Well," he said helpfully, "I bid the club because it's the short club convention."

"Oh yes," I said, being a person who does not like to argue. "I had forgotten about that."

The man walked away wearing a superior smile, and I am sure he has since told the story to every one of his friends and several of his enemies. "You mean you actually explained something about bridge to Charles Goren?"

"I certainly did, Agatha, I certainly did."

Maybe you think I was hypocritical, but I happen to know that this particular man has been playing bridge for thirty years, and if after all that time he still thinks that there's such a thing as a short club convention, not even a regiment of life masters is going to convince him otherwise.

While we're on the subject of bids that should not be bid, allow me to list one more: the "trap pass." This abomination against all the laws of logic, mathematics and decency should be declared a federal offense calling for a mandatory ten-to-twenty year prison term with no time off for good behavior. The trap passer is an egoist who thinks that somebody up there likes him so much that He will reverse the laws of means, probability and chance. The trap passer sits there with 16 points and says "Pass," usually with a croak in his voice and a sly smirk on his face. This instantly marks his bid as a phony (if he had enough intelligence to be a good actor, he wouldn't be a trap passer). At this juncture there are only 24 points in high cards left in the deck, and they are distributed among three players who, mathematically speaking, should be holding hands of about 8 points each. What makes the trap passer think that under these conditions his opponents are going to have enough points to bid up their cards and get into trouble? Don't ask, because I can't answer. I *can* tell you, however, that the trap passer and his victimized partner may well have a game in hand, or close to it. But the trap pass will serve quite nicely to keep them from ever finding out. When the hand is passed by everybody at the table, the trap passer will fling his cards into the center with tremendous speed, and at the same time he will say, "I had 9 points." He is ashamed of himself, poor fellow, and no wonder. The trap pass is about as valuable as the old rule that the cards will run in the same direction as the bathtub. Of the two ideas, I think there is more logic to the second.

3

Successful communication

When modesty is the best policy

If you bid improperly and reach the wrong contract, all the playing skill in the world will not redeem your error. At that point, it's as though somebody gave Michelangelo three cans of spray paint and told him to do the Sistine Chapel. And yet the world of bridge is loaded with people trying to pull off equally impossible feats of card-playing legerdemain. I call such characters playmasters. They are rather bored with all the literature on bidding. They play the game almost entirely for the fun of executing a Vienna Coup or a double finesse with a full twist in the pike position, or something equally complex in the play of the hand. And, bidding as sloppily as they do, these playmasters get a lot of practice making such desperation maneuvers. But it's lost youth. They are never going to become good bridge players. What they really are is whist players trapped in the wrong century.

At the other extreme, logically enough, is the player who has a sole *raison d'être:* to bid. He imagines that bidding systems are totally precise; he has a bid for every occasion and thinks of himself as the greatest genius of communication since Guglielmo Marconi. Here we have the bidmaster, and very often he is a loser.

Why? He is telling his opponents too much.

On the lowest levels of bridge skill, you must run the risk of telling the opposition more than you would like to tell them, because your primary job is to help a shaky partner visualize your holding. But after you and partner achieve a certain level of proficiency, you should be able to bypass some of those minutely descriptive bids and blast on to game or slam more directly. The idea, of course, is to make it harder for the defense to defend, and to avoid debacles like the one that follows.

You're vulnerable and sitting South with this hand:

Partner bids one heart. What would you respond? Three hearts, you say? Precisely. Partner then raises to game and there should be no further trouble. But see what happened when a bidmaster picked up the South hand. To North's opening one heart, the bidmaster responded two diamonds. He could not resist showing his four to the ace. North, who held long hearts but not much else, rebid his suit, and now South checked in with a three-club bid, to show his four to that ace. By now, South and his big-mouth bids had told East and West all they needed to know to make a sacrifice. East was void in North's heart suit. West was void in South's diamond suit and held K Q 9 8 in South's club suit. And between them, East and West held ten spades. So West threw in an exploratory three-spade bid. South, at long last, got around to supporting his partner's hearts, but it was too late. East wound up in a contract of five spades and went down two, doubled and not vulnerable, taking a 300-point penalty but staving off a certain 820 points for game and rubber.

And yet it should have been clear to South from the instant he heard his partner's opening bid that the hand would have to be played in hearts. By the basic rules of arithmetic and bidding, the North-South partnership's best chance had to be in hearts, since South held four to the king in his partner's strongest suit. But South was a bidmaster. Given the most elemental situations in bridge, such players will bid all around Robin Hood's barn for the sheer exhilaration of it, while the opponents sit there re-evaluating their hands, figuring out which of their kings and queens are onside, whom to lead through, what to lead to hit partner's best suit, etc. When the bidmaster doesn't give the enemies the military intelligence they need to make a nice sacrifice, he tells them what they need to know to set the contract.

Are you giving away your secrets?

The bidmaster is usually wholly devoted to ace-showing conventions like Gerber, Blackwood, and that little understood hybrid Roman Blackwood. He will use them even when any further knowledge about his partner's hand can benefit no one but the other team. Let's say he has opened the bidding with one heart on a holding of 20 points. Now his partner raises to three hearts. Chances are the bidmaster will do one of two things: he will start bidding his other suits to show aces, and he will expect his partner to do the same. Or he will jump to Gerber or Blackwood and go through that ritual.

But let's return to the simplicity of the hand. Opener held 20 points, bid a heart, and was raised to three hearts. At this stage, what does the bidmaster know about his partner's hand? He knows that partner holds at least four hearts. He knows partner has 13 to 16 points, the requirement for a jump raise in partner's suit. So the total count in the two hands can be bracketed at a minimum of 33 and a maximum of 36. South, minus drumrolls and fanfares, should bid six hearts. All the ace- and king-showing conventions in the world are not going to result in any other contract, but they *are* going to help the opponents set the hand. Remember, the opponents are on lead; they get first crack at establishing a trick in their own hands. At least half the time, it is the opening lead that makes or breaks a slam. Why help the other team figure the lead out?

The prompt and sudden jump to slam is called "blasting" and there is almost as much to be said for it as there is to be said for the slower, more exacting techniques. The main virtue of blasting is that it keeps the opponents in the dark. It also sometimes puts you in an impossible contract. Never mind. Whenever you have a reasonable shot, blast away! You will almost never be doubled (there are very good reasons why slams are seldom doubled, as we shall see later), and you will be protected over the long pull by that basic bridge axiom: the timid bidder is penalized more than the bold bidder. See how blasting saved this hand:

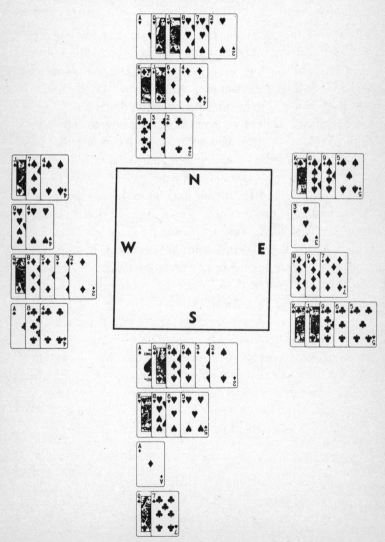

North opened one heart; South bid a spade, and North rebid his hearts. South then blasted to six hearts. A club lead would have wrecked the contract, but the bidding had been so uninformative that East had no way of knowing this. He led his top diamond and now the contract could be made, courtesy of blasting. Slow, cautious "approach bidding" would have tipped off the weakness in clubs beyond any doubt.

All of this is predicated, of course, on knowing your partner. You cannot blast if you entertain the smallest doubt as to whether partner really had his bid. I would not recommend blasting, for example, with the sort of partner described by my favorite quotee, Somerset Maugham: "There is one player whom I have never learned how to cope with, and that is the player who never stops to consider that you also hold 13 cards; he will ignore your bids, he will pay no attention to your warnings, come hell or high water he will take command of the hand, and when he has been doubled and gone down several tricks, he'll ascribe it to nothing but bad luck. You are fortunate if he doesn't smile blandly and say, 'Well, I think it was worth it, partner.' I am still looking for the book that will show me how to deal with him. Shooting is too quick and too painless. . . ."

Years ago, in a Masters Individuals in Pittsburgh, I underwent the Chinese water torture with such a bidder. She had just become a life master, and she was as full of herself as an operatic diva. Coming down the homestretch of the tournament, I was enjoying a comfortable lead when I had the misfortune to draw this woman for a partner. On our first hand I bid spades and she responded two diamonds. I bid two spades and she bid two no trump. I passed and she went down. Two spades would have been a cakewalk. For the next three hands I figured out the right place to play the contract, and in none of those cases was I permitted to play the hand. She went down every time. If I had played one more round with that woman, I'd have called

Willie Maugham and told him to come over with his gun. As it was, I was lucky to win the tournament by one half a point.

"*I told you not to look at your hand.*"

Champions are often guilty of this same bullying behavior but with slightly more justification. P. Hal Sims, one of the top players of the twenties and thirties, used to order certain of his partners never to bid no trump. If the contract was going to be played at three no trump, as if often was, P. Hal wanted to be the player. But he was so good that his less skilled partners were happy to yield to his tyranny.

Not so happy was Mitchell Barnes, a valued member of my international team. Mitch was playing in the Nationals with Charles Lochridge, the two of them making up as jolly, as unpredictable, and as skilled a partnership as you could ever hope to see. But in this tournament, they were getting nowhere, and Charlie came up with a suggestion for changing their luck. "Look, Mitch," he said, "when we come to the next pair of 'rubes,' don't even pick up your cards. Let me do all the bidding!"

Soon Mitch and Charlie found themselves seated against a pair of Life Masters who nevertheless met the Barnes-Lochridge definition of "rubes." Lochridge studied his hand briefly and blasted an opening bid of six diamonds. The opponents were stunned. No one had ever heard of an opening bid of six anythings before. At this point, Mitch figured that Lochridge was carrying bossism too far. Disobeying his partner's explicit instructions, Mitch picked up his own hand, saw four diamonds to the king ten, an outside ace and an outside queen ten. He figured that if Lochridge could blast to six on his own hand, then seven would be a cinch. Mitch bid a grand slam in diamonds and they went down one. "See?" said Lochridge, in high vexation. "I told you not to look at your hand!"

But notice, please, the plain, old-fashioned guts shown by Lochridge in the bidding. The whole idea was a silly one, of course. Mitch's raise was eminently correct, and the failure of the contract was the fault of nobody but Charlie. There remains, however, one lesson in the hand: the experts bid 'em as if they have 'em—even when they haven't. They know that a few penalties suffered from overblasted slams are as nothing compared to a few slams brought home. They also know that a blasted slam is almost never doubled, because opponents don't get enough information on which to double.

Who should play the slam?

And now let me show you something else that experts know about slams: they know *which* hand should play the slam, and they know how to get the contract in the right place. I am talking now about slams that appear equally plausible in either of the partnership's best suits; in a situation, for example, where North holds five good spades opposite South's three small spades, and South holds four good hearts opposite North's four little hearts. Should the contract be six hearts or six spades? Here is one way the experts solve such a problem:

On all big hands, the vulnerable spot is usually the hand with a worthless doubleton or tripleton. No matter that your hand contains a regular Fort Knox in points; that worthless doubleton is the place where you can be set and set quickly, no matter how many points you have. On the other hand, you wouldn't be at the slam level if partner didn't have some high cards, too, and chances are that one or two of them are in that danger suit of yours. So who must play the hand?

Partner, of course. This brings the opening lead *up* to him instead of *through* him and *up* to your worthless doubleton. If he is holding K x or A Q in your weak suit, he is sitting in the catbird seat as fourth player, but he is in a vulnerable position as dummy.

As a simple corollary to this: when you and your partner are heading for slam and your own hand contains a K x in an unmentioned suit, make every effort to play the hand yourself, thus guaranteeing that your king will be guarded against an unfavorable lead.

Now take a look at how this key strategy in the bidding of slams works out in actual practice. South picked up:

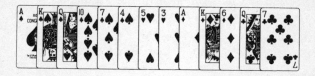

He opened one spade and, to his great glee, heard North respond two no trump. At this point, both expert player and average player would realize that there was a good play for little slam in the hand, and that it was equally plausible in spades or no trump. But the average player, sitting South, would almost certainly bid six spades. Why? Well, for one reason, he's childishly eager to chalk up those 100 honors. And, for another, he knows the partnership has at least eight spades to the A K Q 10, an exceedingly comfortable trump position.

Expert player, however, would ignore both these Loreleis and study his hand. His eyes would become fixed on those two spot hearts, and almost automatically he would bid six no trump. This gives partner the contract, runs the lead through the worthless doubleton and up to partner's heart honor(s). Now let's spread the hand and see the result:

As Li'l Abner would say, "Any fool can plainly see what happens if the hand is played at six spades. The

opening heart lead from West sails right through dummy's
K 9 7, and the enemy takes two quick heart tricks to dump
the contract. But six no trump is ice-cold because there is no
earthly way to attack North's king of hearts with East on
lead. In duplicate bridge competition, I have seen this hand
go both ways: the expert's way and the average player's
way. It is one of the classic hands for separating the new
boys from the ten-year men in the league.

Getting the best result

possible

What to do with an immoderate partner

One of the grand intangibles of contract bridge is: how can you compensate for the bidding deficiencies of a fuzzy-thinking partner and still retain your own sanity and bank balance? Everybody and his cousin has had an answer to this question through the decades of bridge. For a long time some experts have resorted to the homeopathic approach. If you know which way your partner tends to err, they claim, you should counteract him by doing the very *same* thing yourself, i.e. "Underbid with underbidders and overbid with overbidders." Their theory is that the underbidder, observing that you too are underbidding, will tend to reverse his field and become an overbidder to make up for you. I agreed with them on some of their precepts, but not on this one. An underbidder underbids because he is insecure or lacking in card sense or because he is a newcomer to the intricacies of the game, and in none of these cases is he likely to be paying much attention to the way you bid. And overbidding with an overbidder is something I would recommend only to millionaires. If you and your partner can make four spades and you personally overbid it to six spades, you can count on your habitually overbidding partner to go on to seven. This technique would surely convert partner into a more cautious bidder, but in the meantime you both might be on the road to your friendly neighborhood loan company. *An overbidder facing an overbidder produces bankruptcy.*

Some good players, opposite a partner who consistently makes the same errors in bidding, create a University of Contract Bridge right on the spot. The instant the dummy goes down, they frown and begin their lecture. "Oh, I see . . . Hmmmm . . . Yes . . . Well, partner, you *didn't* have that heart raise. Three hearts to the nine isn't good enough support. I don't mean to be critical (a forced smile breaks across the professor's face). I'm just telling you so you'll know the next time it comes up."

Four deals later, partner holds three spades to the nine and raises the professor's opening one-spade bid to two spades. It happens every time. The bridge table is no place for instruction.

What *can* you do about such a partner!

You can adjust your bidding to his idiosyncrasies, asking yourself: "Will partner take this bid as I intend it, or will he miss my point?"

It is important to understand what I *don't* mean by this. I don't mean that you should go out of your way to drop a contract at three hearts merely because partner tends to overbid, or shove a contract up to an unnatural six spades because he is a chronic conservative. And I don't mean "adjusting" your bidding, in any really drastic manner. This is adding your own distortion to the distortion already introduced by partner, and the end result will be chaos.

What your shaky partner needs most is a bidder whose calls are consistent, descriptive, and clear. He needs to hear bids that are not ambiguous—even if you have to lie to make them so. In a word:

> You must make the best bid within the
> limits of your partner's comprehension.

There is absolutely no point in making a big-league bid with a player who will not recognize it. This means that you will have to abandon a grand slam now and then to make sure of a small slam, and a small slam to make sure of a sound game. As the British expert S. J. Simon expressed it in his excellent book, *Why You Lose at Bridge:* "The professional tries for the best result possible. The best result possible. Not the best possible result."

The right bid . . . but the wrong partner

Oddly enough, it is like moving mountains to convince the average player that he should abandon some of his fancy bidding when he is seated opposite a poor bidder. I know players who insist on treating all partners as though they were Helen Sobel, Howard Schenken or—well—me. They throw every super-duper bidding device known to mankind at partners they met just two or three cocktails ago, and then they wonder why they're losing their shirts at bridge.

For my own part, I wouldn't even indulge in a simple cue bid under such circumstances. When your partnership is heading slamward and you cue bid five diamonds to show partner that you're void in that suit, you're taking an awful chance unless you know your partner. Do I hear you shouting that cue bids are unmistakable, blatant, ancient devices, and nobody in your club would ever leave partner in one? Then your club must be the Portland, or the Cavendish—no, on second thought, your club doesn't exist. I have seen players dropped in cue bids in bitter fifty-cents-a-point games, in challenge matches at the smartest bridge clubs, and even in international competition among players widely acknowledged to be the best. To cite a pithy example: in the finals of the Eastern Championships, not many years ago, my opponent Alvin Roth cue bid clubs. His partner, Tobias Stone, appeared not to get the point and so Roth's next bid was another cue bid of clubs. This time Stone passed, leaving Roth in a contract of six clubs, holding a total of five trumps in both hands. As a result they went into a steady decline which permitted my team to win by a considerable margin. Roth's comment was: "I was too fancy, and Stone wasn't thinking." These are two of the finest players in the world, and I tell the story on them rather than some other partnership only because it happens to come to mind. There is hardly an expert who hasn't suffered a similar disaster.

So: unless you think you're as good as Ruth and Stone—but especially if you know you're not—be wary about making cue bids with untested partners. Wait a few rubbers until you're at least satisfied that your partner has an elementary knowledge of such matters—and then wait a few rubbers more.

When you do give a partner a cue bid, and he responds with a pass, and you go down five when you should have made a small slam, whose fault is it?

Yours.

This is one of the many paradoxes of bridge. You made the advanced bid, the "book" bid, the professional's bid. But you made it with the wrong partner. To carry the paradox to its ultimate: when a partnership consisting of a good bidder and a bad bidder reaches an impossibly outlandish contract, it is usually the fault of the good bidder. Often it will go something like this:

A beginner opens one diamond. His experienced partner responds one spade. The neophyte now bids two hearts. This is a "reverse" bid. He has chosen to bid his lower-ranking suit first, instead of the customary procedure of bidding his higher-ranking suit first. This is old stuff to skilled bidders, and means that the player who makes the reverse bid holds a strong hand—at least 19 points.

But two out of three such players will not have 19 points at all. They will not understand the principle of reversing, and their bids will mean only that they have a standard opener and their diamonds are slightly stronger than their hearts. "So naturally I bid my diamonds first!" they will explain later.

The principles of reversing are honored in the breach by most players, and one would suppose that the above-average players would have caught on to this by now. But not enough of them have. When they hear a partner make a reverse bid, they will read him for 19 points and proceed accordingly, even if the partner is in his second week of learning bridge out of an old whist book. At the conclusion of the monstrous contract that usually results from such bidding, the senior partner will fill the air with invective, beginning with: "My God, partner! You reversed, and you only had 13 points!"

"Reversed? Reversed? What's reversed?"

Bridge, too, has its bullies

The contract that got away was not the fault of the player who reversed without knowing what he was doing. After all, he was merely ignorant of one of the techniques of bidding. The foolish one here is his experienced partner. *He* should have known all along that he was playing with someone whose reverse bids had no great significance.

I have a theory about this. To wit: the player who knows the areas of ignorance in his partner's game and yet insists on treating each of partner's bids as though it were coming from an expert is someone to whom winning is strictly secondary. His true motivation is buried deep in the coils of his mind, and it is merely that he wants the glory of climbing all over his partner after the hand and pointing out how obtuse partner was. This sort of bully wants to take the credit and let the cash go, and I, for one, think he has his values turned around.

I once had a friend who personified this type of player. His bids and responses were right out of the book (or at least he thought they were) regardless of the skill or lack of skill of his partner. He would not unbend or yield, adjust or adapt. Thus he was always in a position to correct a partner with less book-larnin'. And he was always broke. His shining hour came when he sat South opposite a partner who held:

With this tremendous hand, North made the atrocious opening bid of two hearts, not only because he was a bad bidder, but also because he was a bad sorter. In the delirium of looking at such a symphony in red, he had placed the ace of diamonds at the top of his hearts, making his hand look like this:

My friend the "Expert" meanwhile held:

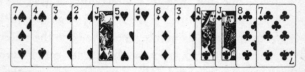

So he responded two no trump, showing less than 6 points.

At this point, poor North discovered his error, gulped, re-arranged his hand, took a sip of his drink and bid four diamonds. South, confronted now with a simple suit preference, bid four hearts.

Tenacious to the end, North went up to five diamonds. South grimaced and put North back in five hearts.

The opponents trumped the opening diamond lead, won the next trick with the ace of hearts, and trumped another lead of diamonds to defeat what had started out to be one of the least settable game contracts in the history of bridge. When it was over, poor, benighted North said: "Why didn't you leave me in five diamonds. I jumped in diamonds and I rebid them."

"I don't care what you did in diamonds," South said. "You bid your hearts first and that means your hearts have to be better."

"But wasn't it obvious I'd made a mistake with my opening bid?"

"I knew you'd made a mistake," said the imperious South. "But I'm damned if I was going to distort my bidding to make up for your mistake!"

Friend South told me about this hand with great pride of accomplishment, as though he had set some sort of new world's record for integrity. I said to him, "— — —, you may go to heaven, but you'll go there in a threadbare suit and unshod. Your bidding was honest, precise, and stupid!" He told me he would resume his friendship with me in thirty or forty years, and, luckily, he still has a few years to go on his promise.

Another friend of mine got caught in an equally untenable position, but this time he claimed that it was all my fault. He was playing with a little old lady who, despite her fragile looks and barely audible voice, was one the reddesteyed overbidders you'd ever be likely to come across. Strictly from *Arsenic and Old Lace*. On this particular night, I was kibitzing the little old lady, and her bidding was forcing me to feats of play-acting—which could be equaled only by the Barrymores—to maintain a straight face. Now I watched her arrange her cards and said to myself, "Well, here's *one* hand she'll never overbid." She held:

Opposite her, my friend opened one heart with:

Without batting an eye, the L. O. L. responded two hearts. Naturally, this was all the encouragement my friend needed to go to four hearts, at which contract he was lucky to squeeze out nine tricks for down one. I tiptoed backward out of the club and caught a cab home, knowing how irascible he could be at times like this. Several weeks went by before I saw him on the street. He ran up to me and without so much as a word of greeting he blurted:

"Do you know what she said when you walked out? She said, 'I knew I didn't have a response, but I hated to pass with Mr. Goren watching me!' That's what she said! *She really said that!*"

My first, unforgettable game with Ely Culbertson

If I've given the impression that I stand aloof from all such bidding debacles, that nothing like this has ever happened to me, allow me to correct the record right now. My files are full of hands in which I was completely fooled by partners who inadvertently made elaborate bids that signified nothing, and other hands in which my own fancy bids went right over the heads of my partners, proving that I shouldn't have made them in the first place. But while I'm talking about confusion in bidding, let me tell you about one such hand where everything worked out beautifully in the end, in the true Hollywood tradition. It is the favorite hand of my life, partly because it is a fascinating juxtaposition of cards, and partly because it happened when I was playing against Ely Culbertson for the first time.

My partner was Sally Young, my favorite partner in the pre-Helen Sobel days, who didn't mind pushing her luck when the occasion demanded, and we were playing Ely and his brilliant wife Jo, at the Park Central in New York. The time was 1938; Ely was the undisputed grand high mucka-muck of contract bridge; and I had just started my own newspaper column. Here is the hand:

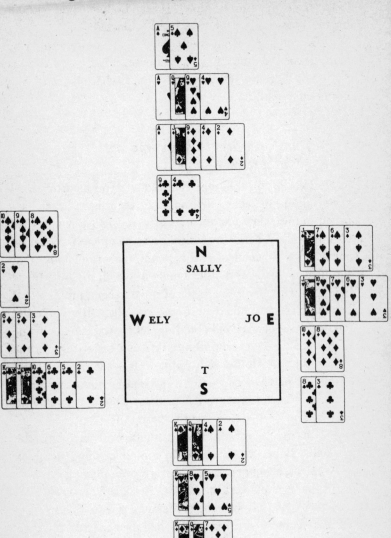

Sally opened the bidding with a diamond. Jo passed. I responded one spade, and Ely threw in a two-club "nuisance" bid. Now Sally bid two hearts, and visions of sugar plums danced in my head. Sally had reversed, showing presumably about 19 points. My own cards counted 19, and the two hands added up to a nice safe-and-sane grand slam. I blasted to seven no trump, and down went the dummy with only 17 points. Sally had pushed our luck a little; we had too few points and too many problems. Our spades didn't figure to run, and our clubs had even less chance of setting up, especially with Ely marked with the king to my left. I didn't know it at that instant, but our hearts weren't going to set up either.

Ely opened his ten of spades, which I took in dummy. I started on the hearts, but on the second round Ely showed out. So at trick four, I led back to the ace of clubs in my own hand and then re-entered the dummy with the heart queen. Four tricks in diamonds followed, and now I was in dummy with one more good diamond to be led. At this point the holdings were:

I led the good deuce of diamonds from the board, planning to discard the dead club queen, and there was consternation in the enemy ranks. Sitting East, Jo was squeezed. If she discarded her heart jack to protect her J 7 6 of spades, she would have set up the nine of hearts on the board and left me with two good spades in my hand. If she discarded one of her spades, she would have left me with three good spades in my hand. No matter what she did, the grand slam could not be stopped.

Ely was enraged. He jumped up and shouted, "God-damnedest luck I ever saw! I've been fixed by Chinese cheap labor!" *

Jo said, "Now, Ely, stop that! Why don't you pay him a compliment? He played the hand beautifully."

Culbertson marched right over to the newspaperman who was ghosting his column in those days. "Record that hand!" he ordered. A few weeks later, the hand, in all its glory, appeared across the country, together with all sorts of complications and conclusions. The main lesson, of course, was clear: there is a divinity that protects the forceful bidder, if he doesn't lose his head.

---

* Ely, always the scholar, was referring to the Bret Harte poem *Plain Language from Truthful James*. The hero of the poem was a Chinese card shark, Ah Sin. "In his sleeves which were long/he had 48 packs/which is going it strong/yet I state but the facts."

The double: triumph,

fun . . . and trouble

If you cannot double, you cannot win

The average person doubles neither wisely nor well—and certainly not often enough. Some players sit around and wait for cinch doubles all wrapped up in guarantees. This is like trying to make one's way in the world by waiting for a rich uncle to die. Others have a built-in radar which tells them precisely the wrong time to double. When the right time comes, the radar set isn't working.

A knack for doubling can make up for many a sin, and a lack of the knack can turn an otherwise competent bridge player into a permanent loser. Over any period of time longer than a few weeks, *you cannot win at contract bridge unless you know when to double*.

All that saves Mr. Average Player is that he is playing against other Mr. Average Players, and they haven't bothered to learn the rudiments of doubling either. Do you think I'm being too harsh on the poor fellow? Well, before you make up your mind, peruse this list of rules of doubling that I've collected:

"Never take your partner out of a business double."

"Never double the opponents into game."

"Never double on the cards you expect partner to hold; double on your own hand."

"Double little slams if you hold two aces; double grand slams with one."

"A double at the level of one is for takeout."

"A double of a new suit is for takeout."

Do you follow these rules? Most of them? *Any* of them? Well, they are all wrong to some degree. And yet these rules, or minor variants of them, make up the average bridge player's approach to doubling. I don't know why. There's never been a book on bridge that advocated any of them. There's never been a competent teacher who taught them. And there never will be, unless someone decides to write *How to Lose at Contract Bridge.*

The trouble with these rules is not merely that they will cause you to make bad doubles, but that they add up to nothing but a weak-sister philosophy of bridge.

I am going to introduce you to a bolder approach, one that will earn you quite a few extra tenths of a cent and at the same time make the game more fun. If you master this method, the Smiths down the street are going to get the shock of their lives the next time they drop in for a relaxing session of bridge.

They are going to spend the evening doubled and re-doubled.

And down.

When not *to double*

But first you are going to have to learn when *not* to double. And the most important double to learn not to make is the one that enables the opponents to fulfill a contract they would never have made without the information given by a penalty double. This is not only the worst type of double in bridge; it is also one of the most common. Our victim holds a hand shaped on this order:

His left-hand opponent opens the bidding with one spade; his right-hand opponent jumps to three spades, and now it is too late for our man to get into the bidding. But he reckons himself lucky, because that poor soul on his left has been led up the garden path and now has taken the contract to four spades.

"Double!" says our hero, and why not? Not only does he

have more than enough points to set the hand, but he also has four trumps to the queen-jack. The hand *has* to go down. And then a funny thing happens on the way to the penalty. Declarer makes the contract with an overtrick and chalks up 390 points of his own—or 490, if he's vulnerable, plus the bonus for rubber.

Oddly enough, our hero's reasoning was correct, to a point. The hand did have to go down, *until he doubled*. After that it was a snap for declarer, for he knew exactly where all the outstanding strength lay. Two finesses through the Q J of trumps rendered those "sure tricks" null and void, and from then on it was just a question of whether he made four spades or five.

There are all sorts of variations of this featured exhibit in bridge's chamber of horrors. There is the double of four unmakable hearts that drives declarer into four makable spades. And there is the double of five spades that (I shudder to say it) drives declarer into a safe small slam in a minor suit—a slam he never would have bid if he hadn't been forced to. I have even seen the ultimate: the double of a small slam that drives declarer into a grand slam which makes. The partner of this doubler was very restrained about it, I thought. He only assaulted his partner with some choice adjectives rather than his bare fists.

The special situation of the powerhouse double

Most blunders of this sort derive from the same specious reasoning on the part of the errant doubler. He reckons that he has to double because he holds so much power. But, in fact, *that is the very reason he should not double.* Allow me to explain this apparent paradox:

When you double on a powerhouse, you are providing the declarer with invaluable information by positioning the problem hand for him. But you might ask: with your own powerhouse, plus the points in partner's hand, shouldn't you be able to set the contract easily? That's just it: *if the other team has reached game in the face of your own 14- or 15-point hand, there aren't any high cards left for your partner to be holding.* If there has been any sanity whatsoever in the opponents' bidding, there can't be anything across from you except, perhaps, an idle jack or queen. (And if there isn't any sanity in your opponents' bidding, you don't need *my* advice on when to double them.) So your double has provided the enemy with information that nothing except a mirror behind you could have provided. Once the penalty double is made, a skilled declarer has located the outstanding strength. Forewarned, he will be able to play the hand in such a fashion that if a squeeze, throw-in, or safety play is necessary for its success, it will be made with absolute assurance.

And he may end up making a contract that was down from the beginning without the double. Obviously, if there is no double, the declarer will play you and partner to hold the outstanding strength fairly well divided between your two hands. This means that he will try some finesses that will work and some that won't. Sometimes he will guess correctly and squeeze you; but he's just as likely to make the wrong guess and try to squeeze partner, who hasn't got anything to be squeezed.

There is no bid that requires so much intelligent thought as the double. The more muscle you have, the more suspicious you should be. After all, your opponents aren't there to throw money away. If they somehow arrive at game in the face of your own powerful holdings, they must have some special reason. Under these conditions, you should believe your ears, not your eyes. You can count your own points exactly, but you can't count the opponents' distribution exactly—*and it is distribution more than high cards that makes or breaks the average contract.*

How many times have you counted A K x x or A Q J x as seven points in your hand, only to find that one of the opponents is void and your fat honors are worthless? How many times have you seen declarer quickly run out trumps and then begin throwing off singletons or doubletons in suits where you hold aces and kings on a long side suit? And how often have you been cross-ruffed to a fare-thee-well? More often than you'd like to remember, I'll bet.

Just to get a small idea of the perils of doubling on your own powerhouse, consider this hand from the Florida State Championships several years ago. Harry Harkavy of Miami Beach was the declarer, and doubling Harry is not one of the recommended ways to get rich. The bidding was peculiar, and the less said about it the better. At any rate, Harry, sitting South, wound up in three hearts. Place yourself in the position of the East player. Against a contract of three hearts, he held:

Not only that, but his partner had put in a spade over-call earlier in the bidding. Was there ever a better time to double? East doubled, and soon found out that, yes, there were better times. Here is the complete deal:

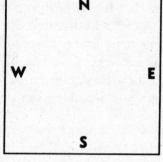
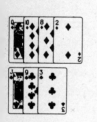

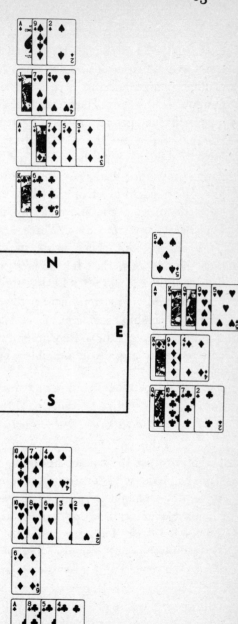

West opened the king of spades, which was won with dummy's ace. Harry laid down the ace of diamonds and then trumped a diamond. He cashed the king and ace of clubs and ruffed a club in the dummy. Then he trumped another diamond in his own hand and another club in dummy! At this point Harry had taken eight of the required nine tricks, and poor East was still sitting there with his five trumps headed by the A K Q. Harry had three trumps topped by the ten in his hand, and the lead was in the North hand. A diamond lead completed the rout. If East trumped low, Harry could overtrump. If East trumped high, Harry could discard a spade and make his ten of trumps on the final heart lead from East. Three hearts, doubled!

I confess that this is a bizarre example of why doublers must be cautious. East felt obliged to double. He'd have been sent back to the Sally League for more seasoning if he had not. And yet he could not set the contract with a combined partnership holding of 21 points in high cards including the top three trumps. Remember this hand the next time you get ready to unleash a double when your own hand is loaded.

Strange holdings and how to spot them

One of the typical causes of poor doubling is the player's inability to use the point-count table *defensively*. Not that point count doesn't allow for this: there are specific rules for evaluating a hand defensively as well as offensively. But not all players are capable of "going both ways" like a star college halfback. They are demons at counting their hand for opening bids and responses, but they haven't a very clear idea what their hand is worth against opposing opening bids and responses. Here your own native intelligence must take over. If you're defending and you hold a guarded king or an ace-queen in a suit, you are justified in looking fondly on them, provided the suit has been bid strongly to your right. If the suit has been bid strongly to your left, your guarded king is probably worth nothing and your ace-queen only one trick. If you hold A K x, or even A K x x, you may be justified in counting two defensive tricks in the suit, but if your partner has bid or supported the suit, the opponents figure to have a singleton or a void in that suit between them so that your ace and king do not figure to cash. If you hold something like A K Q 7 3 or A K Q 9 6 4, you can suspect the suit is worth a maximum of one defensive trick whether partner has supported it or not. And it may well be worth nothing.

The key to learning when not to double is distribution. Many a player will look at 16 points in his own hand and figure, "Well, there are only 40 points in the deck; so my hand means the opponents have a maximum of 24 and probably less." When opponents go to game, this arithmetic specialist will double "on the points." Now and then, against poor bidders, he will have a good double. But all too often he finds himself unstrung by distribution. Too late he realizes that in this particular deal, there were not only 40 points in the deck, but 50 or more, counting short suits, long trumps, dummy points, self-establishing suits, etc. Under these conditions, it is possible for the opponents to hold a game or even a slam in hand despite the doubler's 16 points. Sometimes there are ways to spot these freak situations, if you study your hand and keep your ears cocked. One method is to utilize what Ely Culbertson called the "theory of symmetry of distributions," or, as more plain-spoken players have put it, "One freak, all freaks." If your own hand is a weird one, you'd better make the assumption that the other hands are composed approximately the same way. Even if your own hand is square (no-trump distribution, if not no-trump points), you may be able to spot strange holdings. Perhaps an opponent has opened three or four of a suit, or the opposition has blasted straight ahead to a game contract even though you and partner have been bidding, or they have unhesitatingly contracted for game in a suit in which you're loaded. These are all tip-offs that something is rotten. You *may* have a double, but more than likely this is a 50-point hand with freak distributions that give the declarer many more points than he figured to have on the arithmetic of the matter.

Now it is possible to take all that I have told you about doubling so far and use it to an ignoble end. And that way is to let memorization take the place of your own good judgment. I can hear some conservative player telling his partner next Tuesday night: "Yes, partner, I *knew* I could set the contract in my own hand, but Charles Goren says not to double when you have a powerhouse." Charles Goren demurs. Every now and then the opponents will get themselves into a just plain awful contract, either through unfortunate distribution or bad luck or inept bidding. If it's reasonably clear to you that this has happened, of course you must double. Suppose, for example, as West you hold.

The bidding has proceeded as follows:

North	East	South	West
1 ♥	Pass	2 ♦	Pass
2 ♥	Pass	3 ♥	Pass
4 ♥	Pass	Pass	?

You have a rude jolt in store for declarer. Clearly he didn't expect to lose two trump tricks, and in addition, your diamond honors are placed favorably. Another factor in favor of a double is that neither opponent has shown too much to spare in the bidding which suggests that partner may hold one or two valuable cards. A penalty double is quite in order here. The position of your cards will make the impending profit a substantial one.

However, with the same hand placed in the East position, a double gives too much information away and may provide declarer with the cautious approach necessary to

bring in the hand. In the East position, you have **heard**
South bid diamonds behind you, which all but bankrupts
your holding in that suit. You therefore can count on **but**
three tricks in your hand. It is better to settle for a reasonable expectancy of profit by passing rather than alert **de-**
clarer as to the trump stack by doubling.

The beauty of the probing double

Anyway, it is far more fun to talk about doubles you
should make, and from now on, we shall accentuate the
positive, as Johnny Mercer once put it. Here are a few
doubles that can add spice to your game and money to your
wallet:

Doubles of early overcalls.
Doubles "into game."
Probing doubles.

Each of these is useful, but if I had to say which of the
three is the sheerest joy, it would be the probing double.
Also, it is safe, profitable, and, best of all, you get frequent
chances to use it.

The probling double is a double based on a moderately
good defensive hand and the expectation that partner holds
a similar sort of hand. It is used against game contracts that
have been eked out in such a cautious manner that the
opponents are clearly marked for minimum game holdings
or a shade less. It is a gambler's double, but the mathematics of it are all on the gambler's side. Deal the cards, and
let's see how it works. As East you hold:

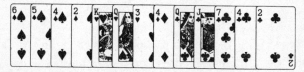

The bidding has proceeded as follows:

West	North	East	South
Pass	1 ♠	Pass	3 ♠
Pass	4 ♠		

The opposition sounds strong, and your best bet is to remain silent. Silence is also golden if the opposition bidding goes:

North	South
1 NT	3 NT

Or:

North	South
1 ♠	2 ♥
4 ♥	

In cases like these, the enemy bidding has been strong and positive. You hold eight points in high cards, but from the sound of things, your partner has little or nothing.

But suppose you hold that same hand and the opposition bidding goes like this:

North	South
1 ♠	2 ♠
3 ♠	4 ♠

Or like this:

North	South
1 ♠	1 NT
2 ♥	2 NT
3 NT	

Or even like this:

North	South
1 ♥	1 ♠
2 ♥	2 ♠
3 ♣	3 ♠
3 NT	

None of this bidding is particularly strong, and, in fact, each of these three sequences fairly well marks the opposition for having a borderline game at best. Usually such bidding will be accompanied by huffing and puffing, searching of the soul, and long hesitations, which you are entitled to take into consideration.

Unless you are facing chronic underbidders (and you should have learned this early in the first rubber), they are marked for a bare minimum—perhaps the necessary points for a game, but more likely a few less.

This is the time to pounce. The opponents have reached game on what may be a proverbial shoestring, and if the lay of your cards suggests that the hand will be unlucky for declarer, make a probing double. To illustrate, suppose, as West, you hold:

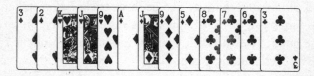

The bidding has proceeded:

South	West	North	East
1 ♥	Pass	1 ♠	Pass
2 ♦	Pass	2 ♥	Pass
3 ♥	Pass	4 ♥	Pass
Pass	?		

You should double!

The arithmetic is simple. Ignoring distribution, you and partner are sitting on about 15 or 16 high-card points. In other words, your partnership and the opposing partnership have equal chance of success. You have barely enough to set the contract; they have barely enough to make it. But *your* points are more or less evenly divided.

This is the toughest possible assignment for a declarer. He never knows which way to finesse, whom to squeeze, how to figure the trump split, and other strategic necessities. Besides this, your heart and diamond honors figure to produce at least the defensive book, and partner is marked with some high cards which may be located in a commanding position. Moreover, you and your partner will get the first chance to upgrade your holdings by means of the first lead; you will be able to reach each other's hands occasionally, and, since the opponents have bid and you have not, you will know far more about their hands than they will know about yours.

Of all the doubles in bridge, this is the one least made, and yet the ingredients for this double are present at least once in almost every rubber. If you don't think so, search your memory and try to recall some of the undoubled contracts you have set. Remember the times you put a minuscule 100 or 150 points above your own line to show that you had set a game contract two or three tricks? Remember all the times you've heard opponents say unhappily, on a routine hand, "Down two." Usually it is on hands of the type we've been talking about.

Observe, please, that the probing double doesn't carry with it the pitfalls of the powerhouse double, where you hold all or most of the defensive strength. This time you *don't* hold all the high cards; you have merely sniffed out a situation where the defensive armament is arrayed on both sides of the table. Nine times out of ten, at least until your friendly bridge opponents begin to catch on to your probing doubles, they will take your double to mean that you *do* hold the powerhouse, which will only compound their errors.

None of this is intended dogmatically, and if you take it dogmatically, you are going to lose your shirt, your house, and your partner. I am not suggesting that you throw everything else out the window and double whenever you hold 8 or 9 points. But do bear the probing double in mind. Evaluate your hand defensively, of course, and if it appears from the bidding that your holding includes queens that can be trapped and long suits that are useless, stay discreetly silent. To put the whole matter in the form of a rule:

> When you have the opposition marked for the bare minimum of points necessary for game:
> Approach a double pessimistically with a strong hand.

Approach a double optimistically with a
moderate hand.

The beauty of a probing double is that the balance of
power is with the defense, even though its points are not
devastating. And something else is working for the probing
doubler: the score sheet. When opponents make a game
against a probing double, they score an extra 150 or 170
points. Once in a blue moon they may even rack up an
unexpected 100 or 200 for an overtrick (but not if you've
made a careful probing double). On the other hand, when
you set them you enter a numerical Shangri-la, expressed in
terms of:

1-trick set	2-trick set	3-trick set
100	300	500

(non-vulnerable penalties)

And even:

200	500	800

(vulnerable penalties)

Where probing doubles are concerned, the price is
usually right. Inevitably, you will have to put up with a
certain amount of oratory from your partner. For years
now, it has been assumed in many quarters that you must
double only on your own hand. The first few times you set
contracts with probing doubles, partner is going to give you
that old cliché: "You're pretty lucky, partner. *You* doubled,
and *my* hand took the setting trick." Sure it did, but off the
bidding, it pretty nearly had to. And you were the one who
diagnosed this, not that ingrate sitting across from you with
the condescending smile on his face. He's the lucky one. He
has you for a partner.

Doubling
  as offensive strategy

There are certain bridge players who are crying out to be taken to the cleaners, and I don't mean this as any reflection on their sartorial splendor. I give you my word: they are there. It only remains for you to find them. I'm referring to:

Those who make overcalls with hardly any points.
And:

Those who make overcalls only to indicate a defensive lead.

When these players put in their nuisance bids, they are depending on an unfortunate fact of bridge life: the average player would rather make game than administer penalties. As soon as many players sense that they have a shot at game, they will treat intervening bids with complete disdain and roll right along toward a game contract. En route, they may ignore overcalls that could be worth three times as many points as game in penalties. Thus they create a vacuum into which the wild-eyed overbidder rushes, secure in the knowledge that his opponents' compulsion to make game will keep him from being left in his own bad bid.

In a sense, the enthusiastic overcaller is an anachronism. He dates back to the early days of contract, when players would overcall on a whim or a fancy, sometimes only because they were bored by having to sit there looking at a jack-high hand. Then the bridge world discovered the effectiveness of the business double, and the zany overcaller soon found himself up to his eyebrows in penalty points. Those were the days of the famous Webster cartoons, which described in vivid terms the fate that awaited the culprit who had the temerity to remove his partner's business double. (A man is being led to the electric chair. An onlooker says: "What did he do?" A guard says, "He took the governor out of a business double.")

The effect of this emphasis on penalties was to stifle the irresponsible overcaller, and he remained stifled for at least a few decades. But my own eyes and ears indicate a trend toward the return of this exiled public enemy. In my recent wanderings from card table to card table around the world, I have been seeing more and more overcalls with fewer and fewer points than in many a long year. Bridge, like the stock market, has its cycles, and my personal poll says we are in another period of risky overcalling. As your bridge broker, I recommend that you take advantage of this market and:
DOUBLE!

To be sure, you won't get as many chances to make doubles of weak overcalls as you will to make probing doubles, but when the chances do arise, they will be gilt-edged. The difference is that the probing double is made against game contracts, and by the time the opponents have bid themselves up to a game, they ought to have a fair idea of what their best suit is, to say the least. But the double of an overcall frequently catches the opponents in anything but their best suit. An intervener will throw in a two-club bid simply to show that he holds five clubs to the ace, and another will overcall just to cut down the bidding space available to you and your partner. When you hear nuisance bids like those, your best course frequently is to abandon your own plans for game and lash out with a double.

Let us say that your partner opens the bidding with a spade. Second hand bids two clubs, and you hold:

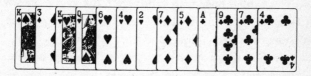

Partner has 13 points, perhaps more. You have 12. Barring some sort of freak distribution, you and your partner are holding five eighths of the points in the deck. But the opponents have already contracted to take eight thirteenths of the tricks! In simple arithmetic, they hold substantially fewer than half the points and agree to take substantially more than half the tricks. The temptation to double is quite irresistible.

The odds will be in your favor

Admittedly, the odds will be in your favor; there are a few ominous possibilities. One is that the overcaller is sitting there with a rock crusher containing eight or nine clubs to the A-Q-J, or that he has only four or five clubs but has caught his partner with half a dozen. Another remote possibility is that your partner, when he opened one spade, was opening a freakish hand himself, one containing few high cards but a long run of spades, all of which makes his hand just about worthless defensively. However, while your double is for penalties, it is based on the assumption that partner's opening bid will produce two and a half to three tricks defensively. If he feels that his hand will prove to be a disappointment on defense, he is perfectly justified in removing the double.

Nevertheless, the chances that partner's holdings will not produce the necessary harvest of tricks are rather remote, and you should double on the assumption that his hand is suitable for defense. To abstain from doubling an overcall for fear that partner's hand may not produce enough winners is an act of cowardice. Moreover, you are taking away his right to participate in the final decision.

You cannot base your bidding on the vague possibilities of disaster inherent in almost any bid. Bidding is based on the science of probability, and the probability is overwhelmingly strong that you will set this particular intervener two or three tricks doubled, or from 300 to 800 points, depending on the vulnerability. Your partner opened and you hold a good hand; there simply are not enough points remaining in the deck for the opposition to get any place. An overcall under such circumstances must start you thinking in terms of a penalty. But first you must disabuse yourself of the common notion that, in bridge, the game's the thing. Seven hundred points in penalties are due and payable in precisely the same currency as 700 points in games and rubbers. And frequently the penalty points are more certain.

In the past, I have reduced some of this to a rule:

> When your partner opens the bidding and
> your right-hand opponent overcalls in the suit
> which you intended to bid, you should double
> for business.

Based on the current trend toward irresponsible overcalls, I would go so far as to say:

When your partner opens the bidding and
your right-hand opponent overcalls in a suit in
which you have some power (a trick or two, or length),
you should double for business.

Before you can cash in on this advice, however, you must be sure of your partner. Otherwise you are going to run into a situation like this:

Partner will open one diamond. Intervener will bid one heart. You will be sitting there with 10, 11, or 12 points and reasonably good hearts, and you will have a perfect penalty double. But as soon as you double, your partner begins to agonize. He squirms in his chair, every now and then giving you a quizzical look, and finally he will bid another suit. In practice, his hand would produce three defense tricks. This is the player who goes by the old non-rule: any double at the level of one is for takeout.

Now it is bad enough to play strictly according to the rules, but to play according to non-rules is unconscionable. So the next time this matter comes up, wait till the rubber is over, take partner aside, and in as calm a voice as you can manage, suggest to him that the purpose of a takeout double is to ascertain his best suit. If he has opened the bidding, why would you need to ask for his best suit? He's already told you. And you can close your gentle lecture with a valid, 24-karat rule:

Doubling as offensive strategy

> Once your partner has bid, any subsequent double by you is intended for penalties and should not be removed unless the opener's hand is totally unsuitable for defense.

There remains one misapprehension to be swept away before you and partner can embark on a glorious career of sending emboldened interveners down to ignominious and doubled defeat, and that is the old canard that you almost never double opponents into game. This philosophy is for scared bridge players. If I were playing some villain with my life for the stakes, I suppose I might hesitate to double him into game. But since bridge is usually played for some smaller wager, such as a fraction of a cent a point, opponents should be doubled into game whenever it becomes obvious that the contract can be set a substantial amount. When does this become obvious? Whenever partner has opened and you hold a reasonably good hand, or whenever you have opened and partner has given you something more than a minimal response. In such cases, it is next to impossible for the overcaller to make his contract. And—heaven forbid!—what will happen if declarer combines a cross-ruff, a squeeze and throw-in, and three or four successful finesses and does make his contract?

Nothing!

The oceans will not rise up and flood the country. There are worse things in heaven and earth, Horatio, than doubling opponents into game and watching uncomfortably as they make it. The greatest of bridge players have had to endure this classic embarrassment, but they also have pulled off more than their share of 500- and 800-point penalties. Bold doubling of low-level overcalls simply has to show a profit over the years.

Permit me to furnish you with an example:
The following hand was defended by my partner Helen Sobel and myself in a recent tournament.

Both sides vulnerable.
East deals.

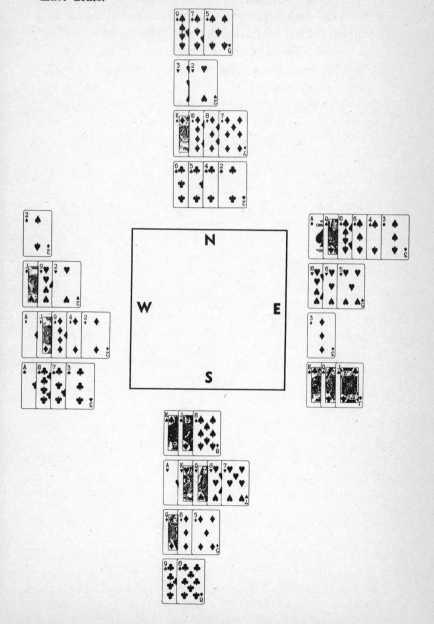

Helen, sitting East, opened the bidding with one spade, and South overcalled with two hearts. With two aces, a few trumps, and a singleton in Helen's suit, I chose to double for penalties, as I did not have a clear-cut bid and game was far from certain. The outcome was quite rewarding—an 800-point sting, as we cross-ruffed spades and diamonds to score our trumps separately.

However, the hand might have been exceedingly unlucky for us, for if this was the layout of the deal:

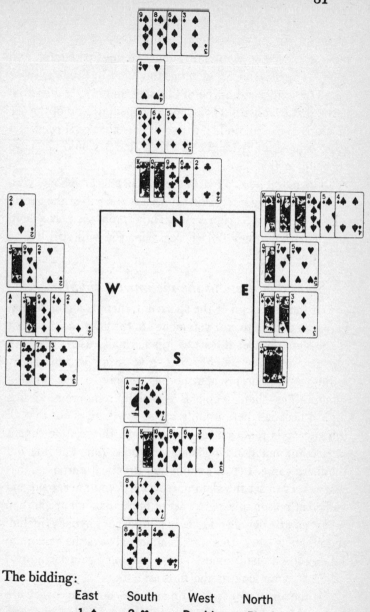

The bidding:

East	South	West	North
1 ♠	2 ♥	Double	Pass
Pass	Pass		

Opening lead: **Two of ♠**

In such an instance, the spade lead would have a mortal effect on our chances. South would play three rounds of trumps, thereby eliminating our ruffing potential, and would actually end up winning the hand by leading twice up to the king, and queen of clubs in dummy. It might be noted that even with this layout, the opening lead of the ace of clubs will still inflict a two-trick setback. However, I must confess with tongue in cheek that I would not have been up to that lead.

The moral here is that if the opponents come home with a "doubled into game" contract, that is the rub of the green. The chances for scoring a substantial profit were excellent, and if perhaps they fail on occasion, you will still live to fight another day.

Slam doubles and the victimized doubler

At the other end of the spectrum, there is a double that is just as certain to *cost* you money in the long run, and that is the slam double, at least as it is normally used. We have already seen how doubles can give away a contract by telling the declarer whom he has to play for the missing honors. The slam double is especially dangerous in this regard because there usually are so few honors out that all guesswork is removed for the declarer. But a more cogent reason for not doubling slams is to be found in the old numbers game. Let us assume, for practical purposes, that you expect to set the slam one trick (if you have good and sufficient reason to expect a set of more than one trick, then go ahead and double and never mind what anybody, including me, tells you). One trick is almost always the maximum set against a slam, unless you're playing against frightful bidders. Now look at the figures:

If the opposition bids slam and goes down one, they are penalized 50 or 100 points. If you have doubled, they are penalized 100 or 200 points. Your net gain by doubling is 50 or 100 points. But what happens if they make the slam?

In a minor suit, they get 170 *extra* points doubled, 410 *extra* points redoubled.

In a major suit, they get 230 *extra* points doubled, 590 *extra* points redoubled.

I have italicized the word "extra" in each case to emphasize that these are points solely attributable to your double; they are in addition to the normal slam bonuses and the normal points for each trick. You don't have to list all the possible combinations of vulnerability and non-vulnerability, overtricks and undertricks, major suits and minor suits, to begin to see what a loser's bet the slam double is. Mathematicians have figured that the average slam double puts the doubler into the position of laying four-to-one odds that he will set the contract. And that simple arithmetic is what reveals the falsity of another non-rule of bridge: "Double little slams if you hold two aces; double grand slams with one ace."

If the opponents reach a small slam with two aces missing, it is true that they may have bid wretchedly. More likely, one of them has a void in some suit, in which case your two aces will amount to a booby trap if you choose to double on the basis that they both will cash. The same goes for players who reach a grand slam minus one ace. You may have them by the scruff of their necks, but is it worth a four-to-one gamble *especially when your double is going to give them valuable information?* Only if you're playing against your boss.

I remember a night on one of my bridge cruises when an average player with delusions of grandeur inveigled Helen Sobel into a rubber bridge game. This is like luring a judo black belt into an alley and telling him to put up his dukes. As that long night waned, the poor fellow began to suspect Helen of being a magician. Over and over again she would bid game against his 15 or 16 points; he would double, and she would make the contract. Or he would double her slams with an ace or two and perhaps an outside king-queen, and Helen would find a line of attack that would render his honors null and void. When the wreckage was cleared away, he took me to one side and said, "Mr. Goren, I can't understand that. I know she's good, but nobody is that good!"

I said, "Did you see the play, *The Music Man?* Do you remember the advice the father gave to his son? He said, 'Son, if somebody bets you he can make the ace of spades jump out of the deck and spit cider in your ear, don't bet him, because you'll end up with an ear full of cider!' "

"Thanks," the man said, and he wandered away, tugging at his ear.

There are two exceptions to the general rule that you should not double slams. The first is my oft-reiterated advice that sometimes the opponents will be so far out of bounds that you'd have to be a Calvin Coolidge conservative not to take advantage of their folly and double them. The second is the so-called conventional slam double, a useful, aggressive convention. The main purpose of the slam-double convention is to set the contract, not necessarily to rack up a fortune in penalties. It is used when it appears to be the best approach to the defense of the hand. Roughly speaking, the slam-double convention calls for an unusual lead. Expressed in rule-book fashion, it asks partner to lead:

> The first suit (other than trump) bid by
> dummy, or, if dummy has bid no side suit,
> the first side suit bid by declarer.

In other words, when your partner doubles a slam, you don't lead trump; you don't lead a suit that might have been bid by partner; you don't necessarily lead your own best suit.

Under what conditions would you use this convention? Suppose dummy's first side suit was clubs and the opponents are now in a contract of six diamonds. You have only a few trumps, and you are void in clubs. A slam double will alert partner into leading a club so that you can trump it with a card that otherwise would be useless. You may not necessarily set the contract, but you've gained one trick you had no other way to gain. On the surface, it appears that you're still flying in the face of four-to-one odds, but this is not the same situation as in doubling with two aces. In the present instance you have every reason to believe that the opposition will make their slam unless partner leads a club. You stand to gain the value of the slam that you expected to lose otherwise, plus the additional bonus of the doubled undertrick. The odds are distinctly in favor of the double, since this time your double has provided partner with more useful information than it has provided declarer, and may even send the slam tumbling down to defeat with the resulting loss of hundreds of bonus points. To put it another way:

> A penalty double purely for enrichment is not apt
> to be of help in defense. And often, it will
> help the opponents bring the slam home.
> A conventional slam double will make the slam
> more difficult to make and may torpedo
> it altogether.

And how do you tell which is which? You discuss it in advance with your partner. If he plays the convention, all slam doubles must be considered a demand for the unusual lead. If he doesn't, then shy away from slam doubles unless they come with a money-back guarantee in writing. You can't beat the odds.

The other side of the coin

Now we have discussed when to double and when not to double, but we haven't discussed how to avoid getting doubled and penalized, nor have we discussed when to redouble. Or have we? If you remember what's been said so far, you've learned plenty about both. Mostly these are matters of gauging your opponents. If you know you're playing against an opponent who doubles strictly on his own hand, you may find the information valuable enough to justify a redouble, especially if you can see that the distribution is in your favor and you're operating with one of those freak deals. Perhaps your hand is riddled with holdings like A Q x x, K J x x, A Q 10 x, and other tenaces. If the player to your right doubles, you might be justified in redoubling, all the more so if you have reason to believe that his is a powerhouse double.

To avoid getting doubled and hurt when you overcall, restrict your overcalls to the land of reality, i.e. overcall not only on the basis of the points which you hold but, above all, a long suit that will be good for four or five tricks regardless of what else is outstanding. You can go down but not often and not painfully.

The question of how not to get set is often the question of how to spot misfits before you're in the soup. Under modern bidding systems, you will seldom get to game or slam without something like the required number of points, and you will usually be in the partnership's best suit. But there remains the matter of fit, and if the bidding begins to show that you don't have a fit, you should run, not walk, to the nearest emergency exit. Never mind that you hold enough points for game; without a fit those points will evaporate right before your eyes. Suppose partner opens the bidding with one diamond. You have a singleton diamond, but you have five spades to the king-queen. So you respond one spade. Partner bids two clubs, of which you have two small. But you also have five hearts to the ace; so you try two hearts. Partner bids three clubs, and now a neon light should be flashing in your mind: M I S F I T

Partner doesn't have your spades or hearts; you don't have his diamonds or clubs. Under those circumstances, the hand is not going to make game anywhere, even in three notrump (which is what many players would bid under these circumstances). You must get out while you still have your savings account. A contract of three clubs is nothing to sing about, but it is better than a fancy game contract that inevitably will go down—and perhaps doubled.

There are other approaches to misfits. Take the standard situation where one player keeps bidding hearts and his partner keeps topping him with spade bids, until finally the contract reaches an unmakable four. Who should have quit? Once, in a lighthearted mood, I wrote that the younger of the two partners should defer to the senior. But I withdrew the suggestion; too many people took it seriously, and there were some ferocious battles in certain ladies' bridge clubs. A better way is to observe this rule:

> The player with the high cards should try
> to become dummy; the player with the long
> suit should try to become declarer.

You can see the logic: the player with the long suit is usually relying on that suit for most of the points he has been showing. If his suit does not become trump, his hand is reduced to ashes. There's nothing as hard to reach as six good spades on the board when hearts are trump. Such a dummy will seldom contain enough entries to enable you to run the spades. Look at the following hand:

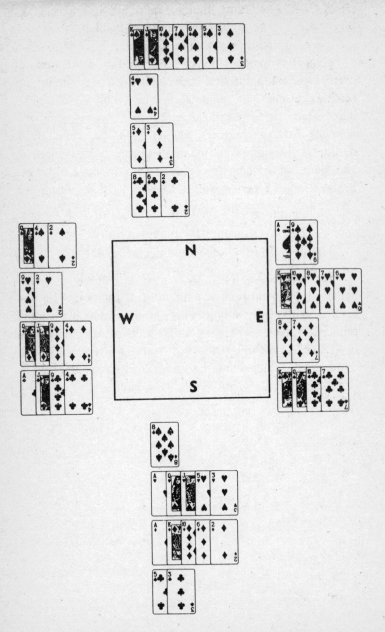

South opened one heart; North responded one spade; South tried two diamonds, and North repeated his spades. South passed. Many a lesser player, holding South's 17 points and ten red cards, would have bulldozed his way to a game contract. But South had the good judgment to realize *a]* that the hand was a misfit, and *b]* that North's hand was largely composed of spade length. His pass enabled North to become declarer and make a safe two spades. Any game bid would have gone down. And so it is with misfits. The higher you go in your desperate search for the right suit, the worse matters get. The moment you smell a misfit, bail out and try to make the high-card hand dummy. Some opponents will twit you for being too conservative. Never mind their gibes and gambols. The aim of bridge is not to bid game and make it, but to *bid what you have and make it*. If you do the second, the first will take care of itself.

The obstacle course
    of conventions

"Explain 'em to yourselves!"

Some bridge players use conventions the way a certain lady used pancakes. She told the psychiatrist that she felt fine but that her family had ordered her to see him. "Why?" asked the doctor.

"They said I liked pancakes too much," the patient answered.

"There's nothing wrong with that. I like 'em myself."

"Oh, you do?" the woman gushed. "Well, you must come right over to my house. I've got a closetful!"

I know players who have a closetful of conventions and a headful of swirling confusions. In tournament bridge I am constantly facing opponents whose lists of conventions reach across the river and into the trees. That's one reason I cut down on my intense schedule of tournament play. It was just too wearying to play against "experts" who didn't know what day of the week it was and yet were announcing all the fancy gimmicks they were going to play. More than once I had to choke back an urge to say, "Don't bother explaining your conventions to me. Explain 'em to yourselves!"

You'd be surprised how many teams take pride in writing down six or eight Rube Goldberg conventions to impress their opponents in tournament bridge. The high point for too many of them comes when they produce this heavy list; after that, everything seems to go downhill as they slip and slide from one puzzling artificiality to another and finally into the oblivion of a low finishing score.

Well, it might be said that it's *their* business if they want to encumber themselves with tool kits bigger than they can use. But it *isn't* merely their business; we're in the game too. They may choose to play all sorts of murky conventions, which is their privilege. But we, as their opponents, are forced to learn their conventions in self-defense.

And that, to me, is painful. If all these new gimmicks parading down the pike were of any lasting value, it might be worthwhile for us to study them. But almost without exception they are useful only for throwing opponents off stride for a brief period.

My advice to you is to scorn just about all of them. Don't let artificialities weigh you down. You can't run a hundred-yard dash in hobnail boots, and you can't reach a proper contract if there are a half dozen artificial bids to be doped out en route. Nor can you have much fun that way. And I cling to the old-fashioned idea that fun is the reason we're at the table.

Are we speaking the same language?

If I were cutting into a strange game with players I didn't know, I would restrict myself to a single convention: Blackwood. And even this old standby can cause havoc. It is used about three times as often as necessary, as Easley Blackwood himself has often pointed out. A lot of players seem to think that it's immoral, not to say illegal, to bid slam without first making the Blackwood calls for aces and kings. Once a woman dropped me at five spades when we held a sure slam. "You didn't ask me for aces," she explained later. After years of experiences like that, I developed a theory about the Blackwood Convention and its overuse. Basically, Blackwood is the pet of the frustrated married woman. She's been led around by her husband, and now she has a device with which to retaliate. She bids four no trump, and that big bully of a know-it-all husband is forced to reply in a predetermined manner. She's got him right where she wants him; she's running the show for a change, and even though she doesn't need to know how many kings he has, she pushes on to a five no-trump call, just to show her authority. (Often as not, he'll hold one king and bid six diamonds; their suit will be clubs; so she'll be forced to bid seven clubs and she'll go down one. But she's already had her fun.)

I can't warn you too emphatically to keep out of Blackwood when you don't need to be there. Remember, there are four other ears tuned to those revealing responses your partner is making, and what they learn may be more important on defense than what you learn on offense. Perhaps the most accurate way to approach the Blackwood bid is to bear in mind that it is not made for the purpose of seeing if slam is there, but *to see if it isn't*. You are trying to find out if opponents can win two quick tricks, not whether you can make six or seven yourself.

Everything I've said about Blackwood is also true of the Gerber Convention. Gerber is merely Blackwood in a special economy package, and as such it can be extremely useful on about 5 per cent of your slams. But make sure your partner understands the bid and the responses. The first time I played with John Gerber he asked me if I played his four-club convention, and of course I said yes. I opened a hand with one no-trump, and he burst right into the four-club asking bid for aces. This was a friendly, informal game; so I started counting my aces aloud on my fingers: "Four diamonds shows one ace; four hearts shows two; four spades shows three, and four no trump shows four." Bedazzled by my own mathematical genius, I bid four no-trump to show my four aces.

And John passed.

"How many did you want me to have?" I asked. "*Five?*"

As the discerning reader has already discerned, I had toted up my response incorrectly. The first step of four diamonds doesn't show one ace, as I had reckoned, but no aces, and the response of four no trump doesn't show four aces, but three. You have to admire John Gerber's integrity; he saw me counting, and he knew I had four aces even though I had bid them improperly. But he refused to press on to slam on the basis of information unfairly attained, and we had to settle for a game.

The moral of the story is that even among those of us who ought to know better, artificial bids can lead to trouble because such simple devices as Blackwood and Gerber are not always fully understood. If you doubt that, answer this question: what is your Blackwood response if you hold four aces?

Did you say five no trump?

About half the players in the world would tick off the responses on their fingers, as I did, and arrive at a bid of five no trump. The correct answer, of course, is five clubs, the same response you would make if you held no aces. Gerber works similarly; a response of four diamonds shows four aces or no aces. It's clear enough when you know how, but *make sure partner knows it too*. Don't be victimized the way John Gerber was with me!

Some classic lapses of communication

The literature of bridge is full of such bidding gaffes, and there isn't a name player alive who is exempt. The English stars Terence Reese and Boris Shapiro were among those burned, and not just in an unimportant club game but in the European Championships. They were playing the "transfer bid," which works like this: if you open one no trump and I make a quick burst to game in a suit, I don't want the hand to be played in the suit I've bid but in the next higher-ranking suit. This gives you, with your powerful no-trump hand, the chance to bid my best suit and become declarer, and makes the opening lead come up to the strong hand. To put it another way, if you open one no trump and I respond four hearts, I am telling you that my long suit is really spades and that I want you to bid spades and play the hand.

By now, I'm sure you've figured out what happened to

Reese and Shapiro. One of them opened one no trump; the other burst to four hearts to show his spades, and the opener left him there. In hearts, the partnership had three or four cards. In spades they had a slam.

Another artificial bid that often results in long lamentations is the so-called weak two opening, the basis of many of the exotic systems currently going the rounds. The weak two opening seems based on the premise that the fewer points you have, the more you should bid, a proposition I do not care to defend. At any rate, the weak two bid was being played by a pair of sharpers in a high-stake game in Miami Beach not long ago. A friend of mine was sitting fourth hand against this pair when he heard the dealer open "two spades." My friend's partner passed, and so did the dealer's partner. All of this was manifestly puzzling to my friend, whose own hand bore one face card: a jack. "Somebody at this table," he said to himself, "must have a reasonably strong opening bid." So he passed, and it turned out that the opponents had a laydown six spades. They had not bid them because the dealer's opening bid was supposed to be a "weak two bid," but in the excitement of picking up a rock crusher, he had forgotten the system and had bid a plain old-fashioned two demand, the most powerful call in bridge. His partner held considerable strength but, not being a mind reader, he felt constrained to pass the "weak" opening.

One can but sympathize with these two players, their lines of communication hopelessly cut by an artificial system of dubious value at best. But what of Chico Marx and the plight he once managed to get himself into? Let us waste no sympathy on that scallywag Chico. He and his brothers decided to sabotage a local bridge tournament by using the submarine system, or the old one-under-one, in which a bid of one spade really means you have hearts, a bid of one diamond really means you have clubs, a no trump means spades, etc. Except for the fact that this system is illegal, it is highly effective—in the right hands. The Marx brothers did not possess the right hands, and after three or four deals they had one another so hopelessly confused that they ran dead last in the tournament. (Perhaps they should have stuck to an earlier Chico system, in which he would sit in the rafters and wigwag the opponents' holdings to his brothers.)

The less you assume, the further ahead you'll be

Sometimes there seems no end to the problems of communication in bridge, and no end to the devices for coping with them. But even the best of such tools require a sound partner, one who will instantly take your artificial call for exactly what it is. A case in point is the conventional slam double. As we noted in the previous chapter, when you make this double, you are asking partner for an unusual lead. *Not* the suit you bid yourself. *Not* the suit you doubled. You are asking him to lead the first side suit bid by dummy, or, if dummy has bid no side suit, the first side suit bid by declarer. For most players, this is quite difficult to remember. If you assume that the average partner *can't* remember it, you will come out ahead of the game.

If you're cutting around in a club game, and you give an unreliable partner a conventional slam double, he will lead your own bid suit without batting an eye. If you haven't bid a suit, he will lead the opponents' unbid suit. Bet on it. Count on it. If your partner is slightly more skilled, and you give him the conventional slam double, a light will flash in his head and he will say to himself, "Oh yes, that calls for an unusual lead." So he will give you a low lead from his own A Q x x x, which certainly meets the requirements of the unusual but will produce adverse results.

If you are absolutely certain that *a*] your partner knows what a slam double means;   *b*] your partner is the sort of fellow who does not make mistakes on such things as who bid what side suit first; and *c*] your partner is only on his first scotch and soda, then give him the old slam double loud and clear, confident that he will lead the correct suit and the grand slam will be set on the opening lead.

Otherwise, forget it.

Another of the current conventions that I find more cumbersome than it is usually worth is the "five-card major," which prescribes that you may not open a major suit with less than five cards in it. With a hand like this:

You are expected to open with your stronger minor, in this case diamonds. On the second round (if there is a second round), you start showing your majors.

This system is not entirely without merit, and I must admit it has a following, but I've never embraced it because I've always preferred natural bidding. When you have a good four-card major, or two good ones, as above, this convention forces you to bid a diamond or a club on hands that really aren't suited for a minor-suit bid. And what happens when you have a legitimate diamond or club opening? It takes two or three rounds of bidding for your partner to realize that you're not kidding him, that you actually do have that minor suit. I maintain that this is two or three rounds too late. The result of the five-card major convention is ambiguity, doubt, overcomplication and lack of confidence between partners, not to mention many more errors than are made in natural bidding. The business of knowing that your partner has five spades or five hearts can be comforting, I'll admit, but if you're a skillful player there's nothing wrong with playing a contract with seven trumps: four in one hand and three in the other. We call this a "Moysian Fit," in honor of the editor of *Bridge World*, Sonny Moyse. It was Sonny who first argued against the five-card major convention, saying that four trumps facing three could produce some fine results. And he proved his point many times over.

The Goren system revealed

Sometimes I wish I could offer, simply for dramatic effect, a flashy, eye-catching convention that would make everybody marvel at my ingenuity. Something like: "A double jump in a red suit opposite an opening two bid in a black suit shows possession of 16 points and a one-eyed jack," or: "An opening bid of one in a suit shows 12 to 14 points sitting North or South and 16 to 18 points sitting East or West, except on alternate Wednesdays, when it shows possession of the six of diamonds."

But I've never been able to invent anything so radical or imaginative. I am stuck with a natural system of bidding, wherein an opening bid of one diamond means—of all things!—that I have good diamonds; wherein a two opening means that I've got a strong hand; a one no-trump opening means I've got no-trump distribution, and other consummate simplicities. I am naïve perhaps, but no more so than the Southern gentleman who once said to me, in what I took to be a compliment, "I agree with you, Mr. Goren. When a man bids clubs, he should have clubs, the way God intended."

Whenever somebody tries to sell me the idea that hyper-complexity is the route to winning bridge, I think of a year when my team was in the national team-of-four championships in Cleveland. We had already won the event once, and this time we successfully defended our title on one of those nights a bridge player never forgets. Our team was in perfect mesh; for thirty-six successive hands we made decision after decision without so much as a hint of error. The second-place team wasn't even close. Afterward came the inevitable remark by the inevitable kibitzer, who, it turned out, had been keeping watch over me. "I don't see where he's so wonderful," she said within my earshot. "There wasn't a thing he did tonight that I couldn't have done." I will never forget that remark. It still stands as one of the warmest compliments of my career.

The excellent British player, S. J. Simon, recalled a similar example of the virtues of simplicity in a duplicate match. He and Harrison Gray had reached a contract of three no trump. There were nine cold tricks in the hands—no more, no less—and they proceeded to take them and run. Later a pair of bidmasters, armed with the latest automated equipment for exchanging information, were bemoaning the fact that on the same hand they had taken five rounds of bidding to reach a contract of four hearts for down two. They wanted to know how in the world Gray and Simon had reached three no-trump on such holdings. The bidding slips were produced, and it turned out that Gray and Simon had bid as follows:

North	South
1 No Trump	3 No Trump

I'm not trying to imply that our results in Cleveland or the Simon-Harrison Gray results in England couldn't have been achieved by some of the bidding systems going around. They could—but only by circumlocutory bidding filled with pitfalls and snares, and only by partners who knew each other's most minute idiosyncrasies. So far as I can tell, the main difference between the so-called Standard American System (sometimes known, not quite accurately, as the Goren system) and the various exotics now blooming in the hothouse world of bridge is that it takes much more energy and concentration to reach the proper bid under the artificial systems, whereas a natural approach to bidding gets you there without even breathing hard. Let me repeat and emphasize: I am not totally discounting the artificial systems with their weak no trumps, their weak two open-ings, their strong one-club bids, and their weak jump re-sponses. In the hands of skilled and experienced partners, these systems usually will get you to the right place.

But they will get you there the hard way.

The one no-trump opening: can it ever fail?

Take that cornerstone of many artificial systems, the weak one no-trump opening. The logic behind the bid is as follows: your own hand is fairly weak, 11 or 12 points; therefore opponents may well have game in hand; therefore a one no-trump opening bid will deprive the opponents of bidding space at the one level. This is neither the best nor the worst logic I've ever heard, but consider the risk you must take. Suppose your partner is flat out of honors and your 11 or 12 points represent the total amassed wealth of both your hands. Now you can get doubled (any double of a no-trump bid, remember, is basically for penalties, not for takeout), and you can wind up sorely injured.

I remember a year when the very superior team of Ivar Stakgold and Leonard Harmon ran into several large sets of one no-trump contracts when they were playing weak no trumps in an international match. An English team, after undergoing the same ordeal in an international competition in Bermuda, came into the card room the following day and asked for attention. "Gentlemen," one of them intoned, "we have an announcement. Our requirement for a one no-trump opening has been 11 or 12 points. We have now increased the requirement to 12 or 13 points." Having shaken the world with this revolutionary change, the team resumed going down in weak no-trump contracts.

There's something about the weak no-trump bid that keeps it returning for encore after encore on the stage of bridge history. It is, in point of simple chronology, one of the hoariest of bids. It was already ancient when certain of its modern "inventors" were not yet born. Thirty years ago, my dentist friend and long-time favorite partner, Dr. Leon Altman, used the weak no-trump opening with gay abandon in our games around Philadelphia. Whenever Doc opened with one no trump, that was the signal for the bidding to begin; we could tell that the cards were fairly evenly distributed around the table. The weak no trump is as durable an artificiality as the Loch Ness monster, and like old "Nessie" is rediscovered every year.

Aren't we forgetting something?

Sometimes it's tempting to suggest that highly artificial systems based on strong bids with weak hands and weak bids with strong hands are merely attention-getting devices aimed at enriching those who present them to the public. All such attempts are foredoomed to failure, as everyone who has tried to change bridge radically surely must know by now. The game simply won't be revolutionized. *Change must come gradually, because bridge is a game of communication and judgment, not a game of fads and contrivances.* If you don't think so, watch some of the old-timers who don't have a system, a convention or an artificial bid to their names. They just sit down, look at their cards, and play. They may count their hands in some private way or they may not count at all, whatever suits their mood. But they know the value of cards; they know that an ace takes a king and a king takes a queen, and they get by. And more important, they have a whale of a time.

By contrast I offer you the recent experience of my British contemporaries, Terence Reese and Jeremy Flint. Before they went to the last European championships, they armed themselves with a system of their own, "The Little Major," to combat the dozens of other relatively private systems they would be encountering. Now I wonder if this wasn't the ultimate absurdity. I don't mean this as a criticism of Reese and Flint, who are both great players. But

doesn't it border on the preposterous that they had to formu-
late an entirely new and artificial system in order to play on
an even footing in an international event? And make no
mistake about it: "The Little Major" system was plenty
new and plenty artificial. On this hand, for example:

The opening bid is one heart (the three hearts to the
nine are the little major; hence the name). The bid shows
one to three hearts, 7 to 11 points, and a five-card minor
suit. That's all I know about it; in fact, that is somewhat
more than I care to know.

I have no doubt that the British were fed up with having
to assimilate the newly improvised systems of their opponents every time they changed tables and hence decided to
give the other players a little memory work of their own.
And the British did win, let me hasten to add.

But did they win a bridge tournament or a mnemonics
contest? I confess I don't know. And what I'm really
wondering is: do you suppose they had any fun?

THE KIND OF MAN WHO
BLOCKS HIMSELF IN DUMMY

©1939. N.Y. TRIBUNE INC.

WEBSTER

Tricks of my trade

Play the cards, not the rules

Who among us has not sat down to a bridge game at an impressionable age and heard somebody say, "Now, Charlie (or Alicia, or whatever), just remember: cover an honor with an honor. Second hand low, third hand high. Lead through strength and up to weakness. Never finesse your partner. Lead fourth from your longest and strongest at no trump. And everything will come out just fine!"

For too many years, those rules were dogma. Then there came a time when disregarding them willy-nilly was considered *the* thing to do. And finally we reached a balance, a period of Aristotelian moderation. Nowadays any player worth his salt (including, of course, all my readers) knows that sometimes you break these rules; sometimes you bend them, and sometimes, in a spirit of recklessness, you even obey them.

A wise man once said that there is a lot of truth in old saws; that's how they become old saws. And so it is with our faithful clichés of bridge. They are invaluable to the beginner, and steadfast guidelines for the advanced player. The easiest opponent to beat would be the one who never obeys any of them.

On the other hand, the *second* easiest to beat would be the player who still follows the old bromides to the letter. There are, surprisingly, a fair number of these antediluvians around, and they are more fun to play with than a sackful of Siamese kittens. The pleasure (and the profit) lies in making plays that appear to follow the book but actually give such unimaginative opponents a false idea of what you're holding.

The proper use (and intentional misuse) of the Golden Rules of bridge is akin to the fine art of quarterbacking. A wizard like Y. A. Tittle would send his right end out on the

same deep pass pattern two or three times, and each time he
would hand off into the line. Now the defensive backs begin
to get the idea that Y. A. was using that deep end for a decoy; so they pay less attention to him and more attention to
backing up the line. *Bang!* On the next play, Y. A. flings
one fifty yards to the "decoy," and the game is busted wide
open.

Y. A. Tittle's counterpart at the bridge table will lead
the queen from a queen-jack several times in a row, in
wooden obedience to the rule "always lead queen from
queen-jack." Then he will pick up the same holding and
nonchalantly lead the jack. The rule-bound opponent will
say to himself, "This time he doesn't have the queen, or he'd
have led it. So I'll have to finesse his partner for the queen."
Finesse fails.

But please note: the deception works only because the
clever leader previously obeyed the rule consistently.
Which brings us to a more or less obvious point:

> An occasional unorthodox play wins; but too
> frequent unorthodoxy must lose in the long run.

Timing and dash and verve are the essence of the
matter. The opponents expect certain consistencies in your
game, and your play should be reasonably consistent, else
you will hopelessly muddle your partner. But if you play the
cards and not the rules, you will find opportunities to throw
the opponents for a substantial loss by doing something
irregular. Here is a simple case in point:

You are leading against a small slam, and you hold a
doubleton king in a suit that dummy has bid strongly. You
know that dummy sits over you with the ace. Was there
ever a king deader than yours? There is absolutely no way
to make it good. But suppose you lead low from your
doubleton king. Immediately declarer has a problem. He
can only lose one trick, and he hasn't the vaguest idea where
that missing king is. If he's like many players, he will as-

sume that you would *never underlead a king;* therefore he will play your partner for it, and go up with the ace. Now your king has returned from the dead.

A lesson in deception

In the catastrophic event that the declarer outthinks you and refuses to play the ace, what has happened? You have lost a king that you always had to lose. You were, in fact, taking the only line of play that offered the slightest hope. If it works once in a hundred times, you're ahead of the game. In my experience, it works far more often, as this hand from a major tournament shows:

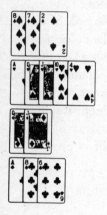

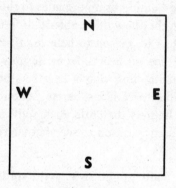

In the bidding, West mentioned hearts twice, showing beyond any reasonable doubt that he had the outstanding honors. East bid spades strongly, and the final contract was six spades.

Now view the hand from both sides of the table. On the defense side, South is fairly certain that he has one good trump—the jack. From the bidding, it has been apparent that East, the declarer, has the top spades. But it is equally apparent that South's king of hearts is going to be trapped by West's loudly advertised heart strength. Unless . . . South underleads his king of hearts.

Now view the hand from the declarer's point of view. With a combined holding of nine spades to the A K Q, he is full of confidence that he will be able to drop the outstanding trumps; he has no reason to believe otherwise. So declarer plays the ace of hearts from dummy's hand. He knows that the outstanding king of hearts will now take one trick, but every other trick is his, barring an outlandish split in trump. Well, he gets the outlandish split, and down he goes. This puts us in position to see another rule of deception:

> When you want to get away with something,
> strike quickly.

If South does not make his tricky move at the opening gun, declarer soon finds out that the trumps are 4–0. This forces him to try the heart finesse in desperation. It works, and he makes his slam.

There is a slight variation on underleading kings that often misleads unwitting opponents. Suppose you are on lead and you hold K J x or K 10 x, knowing that next-hand has the remaining honors. By leading the jack or the ten, you may give the opponent the fearful feeling that you are leading a singleton, and that he must play his ace now or kiss it good-by. What he is actually kissing good-by is his chance to capture your king. Once again, pull this maneuver with the speed of a cobra. With each succeeding trick,

the declarer gets to know more and more about the holdings, and soon he is going to have your hand figured out. By
that time, all the deception in the world isn't going to fool
him.

I'm ashamed to confess it, but all this adds up to a lesson
on how to become a thief and a liar. You will become a thief
of tricks, stealing what is not properly yours, and you will
become a liar because you will play cards that seem to say
something they do not. Bridge is one activity where stealing
and prevaricating are not only approved but pleasurable.
What a difference there is — in sheer fun — between a staid,
set game where everybody follows the old axioms automatically, and a wide-open razzle-dazzle game where nobody
can count on anybody to play in a predictable pattern. Just
suppose, for example, that you're the declarer at a contract
of three no trump, and as soon as the opening diamond lead
goes down, you can see that you're dead if the opponents
attack your hearts. So you run off a few tricks in your strong
suits, and then you nonchalantly lead a heart! "What have
we here?" says a skilled opponent to himself. "That sly old
dog is trying to set up a trick in hearts." This thinker gets
on lead and a heart is the last thing he'll play. And you, my
friend the liar, will make your contract.

I knew a man who advised that you should whistle
softly under your breath while making such suicide leads.
There he would sit, warbling a merry tune, his face a study
in confidence and nonchalance, and his opponents would
figure that he had the contract cold. He got away with some
wildly confusing leads until the other members of the club
caught on and developed a countermeasure of their own. As
one of them expressed it, "When that son of a gun whistles
while he's making a lead, return his suit as fast as you can!"
I don't know what ever happened to this man; probably he is
dealing three-card monte on a riverboat and whistling his
head off.

Finesses I have known

A move that is akin to this chicanery is the phony finesse, which has a thousand different forms, all of them effective against rule-book opponents. When you play a contract, never forget that you can see all of your cards, but each opponent can see only half of the defensive array. Therefore it is easy to deceive them into thinking you're trying a finesse when in fact you're committing grand larceny. Take a hand like this:

$$\text{J 10 6 2}$$

$$\text{Q 9 8} \qquad\qquad \text{A 7 5 4 3}$$

$$\text{K}$$

Your other suits present no problem, but you would like to make that king good. Do you lead low from dummy and hope that East will duck? That might work, but a better approach is to encourage East to duck by giving him a false impression. So you lead the jack. If you will cover up the South and West hands, you will see what this lead looks like to poor East. It looks exactly like an attempt to finesse against the queen. East reasons that the finesse has to lose, and his ace will be good for another trick later. You have duped him into ducking; your king takes the trick, and you lose *nothing* in the suit, thanks to the finesse that wasn't.

There is no move in bridge that provides as much unalloyed joy as the finesse. It comes in handy in the classical sense, when you are trying to trap an outstanding honor, but it comes in just as handy in the larcenous sense, when you are trying to sell some unsuspecting opponent the Brooklyn Bridge. It can even be used to beat coffeehousers at their own game. Years ago I was playing against a wealthy Philadelphia dowager who needed to win in our tenth-of-a-cent game as much as a Croesus needs contributions of old clothes. I was playing a slam hand, and after the opening lead the woman handed her cards to a kibitzer and said, "Here, play these for me while I go to the ladies' room." As it happened, I was trying to figure out which way to try a two-way finesse against the missing queen of trump. When the aristocrat handed her cards to a kibitzer, I jumped to the naive conclusion that her hand was a bust. And as you've already guessed, she held three trumps to the queen and I went down one. After that, I developed a trick of my own to handle people who try to coffeehouse you into misplaying your finesses:

First you select a suit in which you have all the top honors, something like this:

Q 10 6 4

A K J 7 3

You lead the queen from the board, and you watch the next player closely. If he puzzles and frets and stews about his play, you know he's a coffeehouser because you know he has nothing to puzzle and fret and stew about. He is merely trying to give you the old Chase & Sanborn and make you think he has the "missing" king. So you write this down in your mental notebook and from then on you know how to read him when you *are* finessing. Later the cards come up like this:

A 8 7 4

K J 10 3

You lead low from the board against this same player and he slams down a small card without any hesitation. Now he's trying to flim-flam you into thinking he *doesn't* have the queen; therefore you play him for it and win the trick with the jack in your hand. Conversely, if this same coffeehouser goes into a dark trance over your low lead from the board, you must play him not to have the queen; you win the trick in your hand and finesse against the other opponent.

There is absolutely nothing unethical about your play (although there is about his). In trying to guess the location of a finessable card, you may take advantage of any clues provided by your opponents. P. Hal Sims always played the finessable card to lie in the hand of the opponent who talked first, or tied his shoe, or ordered a drink, or hummed. Zany as it sounds, Sims almost invariably guessed where the card was. He became so renowned for this uncanny ability that a pair of opponents rigged a deck so that each of them held the same finessable queen. After a few plays, Sims flung his cards down and announced: "There's something wrong here. Both you pigeons have the queen of clubs!"

Wilbur Whitehead, one of the champions of the 1920s, once used a more direct technique than Sims. Playing against two women who were rendered giddy by the pleasure of his company, he turned to one and said, "You look like a lady with the queen of spades."

Said the woman: "Oh, Mr. Whitehead, aren't you wonderful?"

There are more theories about how to find the finessable card than there are patents on perpetual-motion machines. When I used to play in Philadelphia, an esteemed colleague came up with this wild rule: if you have no clues whatsoever, finesse toward City Hall. Another approach, only slightly more logical, is to play the queen to lie over the jack, i.e. if North hand holds the jack, East will hold the queen. The "reasoning" is that the queen may have fallen on the jack during the play of a previous hand, and imperfect shuffling has left it there. You'd be surprised how many would-be finessers go by this rule and how seldom it works.

The wise player throws out all such gimmicks and tries to guess the two-way finesse in a more rational manner. Now and then the problem will take care of itself; the missing card *must* be in a certain hand or the contract is down anyway. Under those conditions, you have no choice but to finesse in the direction determined by the cards. But if you do have a choice, remember this: The person with the greater number of cards in the suit is the one more likely to have the card you're finessing against.

If East figures to have one or two spades and West figures to have three or four, look for the queen of spades to be with West. You won't be right every time, but you'll be right often enough to make you glad you learned the rule. All of this is easy, but what is not so easy is how to determine who is holding the larger number of spades. And that little problem takes us into a far-out land where most bridge players never venture: the land of "counting."

My short cut to the count

Counting a hand * is something that some people can do almost without thinking and others can never seem to master. It always comes as a shock to the average player to sit down with experts and find that after a few tricks everybody at the table knows his hand. Once a player came to me and insisted that Helen Sobel had some way to read his cards. He told me: "I made my second lead and she said, 'Why didn't you bid? You had an opening bid.' The hell of it was I *did* have an opener, but all I had led so far was a king and a nine."

Counting is an occult art in which not more than 10 per cent of the world's bridge players are proficient, and it is not an absolute prerequisite to winning bridge. The ability to stop midway in a hand and calculate with Sobelesque precision exactly how many clubs, diamonds, hearts, and spades have been played by North, South, East, and West, what cards remain in which hand, and what cards have dropped from each hand, is very much like the talent for being able to juggle six balls, whirl a hoop around one ankle, balance atop a pony and sing "Melancholy Baby," all at the same time. For my own part, counting has never been my spe-

* "Counting the hand," used in this sense, refers not to point count, but to the distribution of the hands around the table and the positioning of the honors.

cialty. Obviously, I know how to count hands, and I will do so if there's no other way out. But mainly I am lazy, and this has led me to use certain shorter cuts toward getting the count. I don't mean the kind of "short cuts" that have been used in the past. In the 1930's somebody came out with a bridge table containing fifty-two buttons in front of each player. Every time a card was played each person would push the corresponding button, and thus the hands would be counted. This gimmick made a foursome of bridge players look like a quartet of accordionists, and it soon fell of its own weight. Then along came "memory decks." Each time you played a card from your own hand, you replaced it with the same card from a memory deck, and thus you always knew which cards you had played. It was easier than carrying hod, but not much, and memory decks died a quick and merciful death.

A more dependable approach to counting the hand is to learn a few basic facts and then back them up with that native intelligence I keep talking about. First, some probabilities:

When there is an even number of cards out against you, they probably will not break evenly. When there is an odd number of cards out against you, they probably will break as evenly as possible.

With those two facts firmly in mind, you will be in a position to start counting hands the next time you sit down to play. But these rules will be worthless without some help from you. Suppose, for example, there are five hearts out against you. The rule says that they will break three-two, and they normally will. But if one of your opponents has bid spades and diamonds, there isn't going to be much room in his hand for hearts, and chances are you won't get your three-two split. In spite of this simple, common-sense reasoning, most players will barge ahead, blissfully counting on the split prescribed by law. What they forget is that the probabilities vary with the bidding, and on a hand like this one you had better prepare yourself for a four-one or even a five-zero split. That's what I mean by using your head. Somewhere in bridge's galaxy of unnecessary complications is an obscure rule that bears on this sort of thing. It says that a player who bids two suits and supports his partner in a third must have a singleton or a void in the fourth suit. You're welcome to that rule if you like the sound of it. But I prefer the approach of simple logic: if you hear a man bid two suits and support his partner in a third, you shouldn't need to lean on a rule to see what's coming. With that bidding, it's all but impossible for him to have more than one card in the fourth suit.

I advise you to stick with those two rules I gave you: *even cards won't split; odd cards will split as closely as possible.* Then you will be prepared to play holdings like this:

A K Q 4 3
5 2

What approach would you take to this holding? It's a rare bridge player who wouldn't lay down the ace, king, and queen, looking for a three-three split. But a three-three split occurs only thirty-six times out of a hundred. That leaves sixty-four times out of a hundred when your play would be disastrous. Following the probability that the suit won't split, you should concede the first trick by playing small from both hands. After that you are all but certain to take the optimum four tricks.

Similarly, you hold:

A K J 6
5 4 3 2

You don't play to drop the queen; you try the finesse, of course, following the ancient adage about finessing: "Nine never, eight ever." But do you know the logic behind the adage? There are five cards out against you, and they figure to be split three-two. Furthermore, the missing card (in this case, the queen) will probably be in the hand that holds three. Therefore, the lead of ace and king will not drop it. Ergo, finesse!

But what if you hold:

A J 10 2
K 9 7 4

Again you start with the assumption that the break will be three-two, but from that point you're on your own. You can finesse either way, and you are going to have to stop and review some of the facts about the hand. Let's say you hold the above cards in hearts. If one player has bid spades aggressively, he probably is long in spades and, therefore, proportionately shorter in hearts. If one player has bid clubs and diamonds, you may mark him as the one who is shorter in hearts. Thus you get some indication of which way to finesse. If you're an astute observer of human nature, like P. Hal Sims, you'd do neither. You'd just wait to see who speaks first.

Another short cut to figuring out the holdings around the table is our old friend, the "Theory of Symmetry of Distributions." If you have a singleton, presume there is another singleton somewhere. If you have a seven-card suit, somebody else is likely to have one. It all sounds absurdly elementary, but the fact remains that many players will pick up a seven-six freak or a six-six-one freak and then play their cards as though everybody else at the table is holding a square hand. Then they will curse the gods of distribution when they lead an ace into an opponent's void and go down one.

The subtle art of playing blind

But what if there is no way to count the enemy hands? Neither opponent has talked, nor bid, nor grimaced, nor even put in a hesitation bid or a significant cough. *Then*

*pretend that the missing honors are where they would
have to be in order to make the hand, and proceed accordingly.*

You may hold in trumps:

6 4 2

A K 10 9 8

Assuming that there is no other way to approach the
hand and absolutely no hint of the opponents' holdings,
lead low from dummy through East. If East holds both the
queen and jack of trumps, you will make all the trump
tricks. The worst that can happen is that they will turn out
to be with West, in which case you had to lose them anyway.

Or you may find that the only way to make the contract
is, say, to play East for a singleton king and West for the
other three cards in the suit. If you're dead certain there is
no other way, play to drop the king. It will work only once
in a great while, but then you'll have something to talk
about for a month. The opponents will say you were lucky,
and they will be right. But at least you had the good judgment to buy a ticket on this particular long shot. You will
not have counted the way the hand was, but the way it *had
to be* in order for you to be successful.

The same technique can work on defense. Take those
awful hands where the opponents carefully bid their way to
a game contract, and then dummy turns out to have 13 or 14
points instead of the bare minimum he has been indicating.
Now the declarer not only has all the points he expected
from dummy, but 5 or 6 more, and a defense looks hopeless.
In such cases, I sniff around for some bizarre play, some
strange distribution that will give them a run for their
money. There's one such hand on the following page:

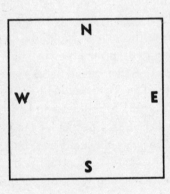

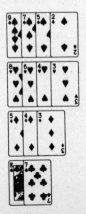

The bidding.

West	North	East	South
1 ♥	Pass	2 ♦	Pass
3 ♦	Pass	5 ♦	Pass
Pass	Pass		

The opponents have gone to five diamonds, and before West lays down his dummy, you as South are grateful that they aren't playing six. You're about to throw in the hand and call for a newer and friendlier deck, when it suddenly occurs to you that there is a way to conceivably set the contract. Suppose—just suppose—that North holds the ace of clubs. Against the strong bidding of your opponents, nothing seems less likely, but on the other hand, what other avenue of hope is there? So you make what would ordinarily be a bush-league lead: the king of clubs. If the opposition holds the ace, you have handed away the one possible trick you have, and they will make six or seven. But look what happens: your king of clubs holds; you lead your last club, which partner takes with his ace; he leads a club back to you and down goes the contract. Once again, you have not counted the hand; but you *have* figured out the one possible distribution that could set an otherwise cold contract.

A blood brother to this sort of attack is the let-'em-make-a-mistake approach, which comes up on hands that are just about hopeless. There isn't so much as a whisper of a prayer that you can set the contract, unless the opposition blows sky-high. So give them their opportunity! You'd be surprised how often the declarer will block himself from the board, or try a totally unnecessary finesse that gets him in trouble, or make some obscure safety play based on heaven only knows what aberrations in his mind. I knew a player who would explode if his partner gave up on a hopeless hand and threw it in. "That's criminal," he once said to me. "Doesn't that partner of mine know the other team can make mistakes? Why, *they might revoke!*" Waiting around for the opposition to revoke is not my idea of the perfect defense, but I must say I admire this fellow's spirit.

We must also face the fact that this business of hoping that the opponents will blow the hand can work both ways. I have seen frightful mistakes that worked out better than the correct line of play would have, as in this hand:

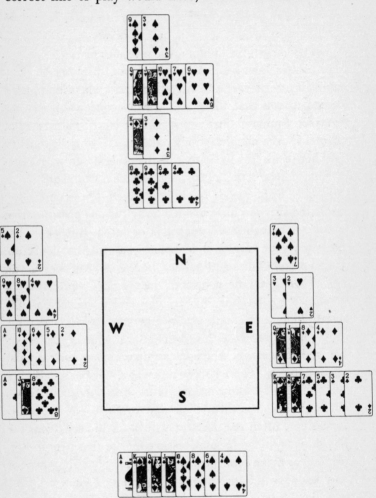

There were three passes to South, who made the as-
tounding bid of seven spades. West doubled and led the ace
of diamonds, setting the contract one. As South ruefully
explained to me later, "If he had led his ace of clubs I would
have made it." Well, against me South *would* have made
the hand, despite his poor bidding. Sitting West, I would
have realized that the declarer must have had at least one
void to open seven spades missing two aces. Now I would
look at my hand and try to figure out where the void was
most likely to be. Since I held five diamonds and only three
clubs, I would mark him for the diamond void and lead the
ace of clubs, and he would then rattle off thirteen tricks.

The next time one of the many stuffed shirts of bridge
starts explaining to you what an exact science the game is,
show him that West hand and ask him what he would lead
against a seven-spade opening bid. You are bound to run
into at least one who will make a pronouncement to the
effect that "You would never lead the diamond ace. You
would always lead the ace of clubs." Then you can flash the
whole hand at him and, citing the good Viscount Grey of
Fallodon, finish off your lesson in humility with:

"There is only one theory about [bridge] in which I
have perfect confidence, and this is that the two words least
appropriate to any statement about it are the words 'always'
and 'never.'"

Lord Grey was actually talking about fishing, but I
warned you that this was going to be a lesson in lying.

Table tactics
of a game for four

Bridge is one part psychology

Is there a more distressing sight than a bridge player who is absolutely certain that he is the poorest at the table? He fusses and fidgets out of fear that each play has some secret meaning that only he, in his shameful ignorance, fails to understand. And between trying to decode obscure meanings and twisting in his innate insecurity, he produces a series of plays you would have to call "dogmeat." Put this same fellow in a game down at the Elks Club, where he has played a thousand times before and where he knows he is as good as the next brother, and he commits no such atrocities. He makes his *own* errors, to be sure, the same errors he has been making all his life. But he adds no new ones based on nervousness.

From this, doesn't your behavior toward partner become obvious? *Treat him like the champion he's not.*

Of course, if you have always recognized that the purpose of bridge is fun, you won't need this advice. You will naturally take a tolerant approach to your partner's idiosyncrasies, because you will recognize instantly that any other approach is going to take the fun right out of the game for everybody.

But treating your partner like a human being is also the most rewarding method, no matter what your reason for playing bridge. Maybe you are playing for material gain . . . or to influence the boss . . . or to show the neighbors what untapped resources of intellect you have. These are all poor reasons for playing bridge, but that's your business. The fact remains: gentle treatment of your partner will improve your score. As some of the leading pros have maintained for years, a big smile toward your partner at the beginning of every session is worth at least 200 points per rubber.

Sometimes it takes an iron determination to put up with

a shoddy partner, but you'd better do it. Every now and then a strange partner will finish butchering a hand and say to me, "Could I have made more?" and I have to fight down a burning desire to say, "No, not the way you played it." But I bite my tongue, having discovered long ago that it is wiser to say something soothing, some little white lie like, "You played it quite well, partner," or, "You got some tough breaks in the distribution." Sometimes a partner will play a hand at two spades and make three when he should have bid four and made five, in which case I'll say something like, "Nice stop, partner, we'd have been down at a game contract." It'll take us four hands like that to make rubber, but if I tell him the awful truth about his game, he will become jittery and we'll be lucky to get up from the table with anything at all.

The same is true of bidding. I've had people raise my opening bid when they had next to nothing themselves, and when dummy goes down, they'll say, "Well, I was told you were a good player." I suffered through a long evening with a partner like that, a little old lady who in all other ways led an entirely exemplary life. When she raised my one spade opening bid to two spades on a hand highlighted by the queen of hearts and a singleton nine of spades, I commented, "Your response to my opening bid was one of the most delicate compliments I've ever been paid." There was the trace of a barb in that remark, and I would not have made it except that I knew she wouldn't catch on. Nor did another player, given to prolonged hesitations, to whom I once said, "Madam, that second hesitation was definitely an overbid." If the urge to make such sarcastic remarks simply overwhelms you, I hope you are playing with partners who won't get the point. With all other partners, you must obey Dorothy Dix's admonition. A woman wrote the venerable columnist that she had found a man she loved and they intended to get married, but she wondered if she should tell him about her false teeth. Answered Miss Dix: "*Keep your mouth shut!*"

You can find profit in a poor partnership

The mark of a first-rate bridge player is not, as so many second-rate bridge players seem to think, the ability to instruct and enlighten an inferior partner at the table. This is the highroad to disaster; for every lesson that you get across to a nervous partner, he forgets six other lessons that he had already learned. The bridge table is probably the worst educational forum ever devised. Under the pseudo-friendly gaze of the opponents, the neophyte takes his lesson (and his medicine) from the superior partner, and then is expected to go and sin no more. Meanwhile, his hands are shaking with nervousness and his head is awhirl with rules and regulations and he wishes he were home reading a light novel.

No, the mark of a first-rate bridge player is the ability to *profit* from the mistakes of the poorer player, and not merely as his opponent but also as his partner. The first rule of coping with a mediocre partner is:

> Learn his game, and, within the bounds of
> sanity, adapt your game to his.

There is even a certain advantage in having a partner who makes the same mistakes over and over. If you're paying attention, you will quickly learn what those mistakes are, and your opponents won't. And often you will be able to turn his mistakes to your own profit. But if you start educating him at the table, what will happen? He'll try to correct his basic errors; sometimes he'll succeed and sometimes he won't, and nobody will have any idea what he means from that moment on. At least, *you* used to understand him.

Back in the dear dead days beyond recall, I played with a man who could not get it into his head that the lead of a king showed possession of the queen or the ace. The first time I played with him, I paid dearly. But instead of screaming at him, I saved my mental effort for studying his game, and soon I had him down pretty pat. Whenever I cut him as a partner afterward, we were a pair of deceptive demons. He would lead a king. Next to him would be a perfectly innocent victim holding the queen. He would duck, and his partner would win with the ace. But would the opponent now lead back to that good queen on the other side of the table? Of course not! Hadn't my partner led the king, and didn't that show that my partner held the queen? And when the lead came around to me, would I return my partner's suit? Not on your life. Any other partner would have the queen, but not mine. The result was that the opponents were kept off balance, and often as not they would fail to cash their good queen at all.

Signaling is another technique with which an inferior partner can be manipulated to your own advantage and the opponents' sorrow. But before you can cash in, remember this:

> Don't make legitimate signals to a partner
> who doesn't read them. You will be signaling
> only for the benefit of your opponents.

Signaling is an obscure art to most players, like sword-swallowing, and the best approach is to assume that partner's knowledge is limited to high and low discards. Even that could be assuming too much; you may have cut yourself a partner who plays the late Chico Marx's convention: "If you like my lead, don't bother to signal with a high card. Just smile and nod your head."

With a partner who is a total loss on signals, you may practice the fine art of the non-signal, or the signal-that-isn't. Let us suppose that you cannot set a contract unless the declarer leads a club. So you discard a low club the first chance you get, telling partner *not* to lead a club. Partner, of course, is blind to this signal, but the opponent isn't, and he rushes in to take advantage of your club "weakness." You can use this non-signaling technique to mislocate aces, indicate singletons and voids when you don't have them, and in general cast the opponents adrift in a sea of doubts.

The same sort of deception, based on partner's ignorance, can be practiced on opening leads. Suppose you are leading against three no trump, and your best suit is A K 9 7 2. A lead of the two indicates that you are leading from a four-card suit, and might induce the declarer to misread the hands and adopt an incorrect line of attack. But your lead might also discourage a skilled partner from returning your suit when he gets in. So you reserve this play for a partner who doesn't read cards as well as your opponents. The lead of the deuce will mean nothing to your partner; he will blindly return your suit, and you will have declarer in a difficult position, not because your partner is bright, but because he is the very opposite. That's what I mean by turning the foibles of a deficient partner to your own advantage.

A special kind of demon: the tyrant

What you can do about the superior partner, or the partner who *thinks* he's superior, is another matter entirely. You can never turn him to your own advantage, and all too often you can't shut him up either. One way to handle him is to excuse yourself, grab a coat, and go out the back door. I have friends who have practiced that strategy, but it has one drawback: it does break up the bridge game. Others, like Elmer Davis, have put up with such partners and later given vent to their feelings in print. As he wrote in *Harper*'s three decades ago: "The persons who feel it necessary to conclude each hand with a magisterial correction of their partners (and perhaps their opponents as well) have no place at the bridge table, or anywhere else where they might come into contact with civilized beings." As usual, Davis was on target, but unfortunately the tyrants he was talking about are with us to stay, as history has clearly shown, and the sooner we learn to adjust to them, the better off our game is going to be.

The bridge tyrant is a person who plays the game for the very opposite of the normal reasons. It has never occurred to him that bridge is fun, or supposed to be. He is like the golfer whose blood pressure goes up twenty points because the foursome ahead is playing too slowly or the basketball fan who tries to take a poke at the referee. If you ever tapped these people during their paroxysms of annoyance and had the nerve to ask, "Excuse me, but are you having fun?" they would merely give you a perplexed look. They are not there to see what is right and enjoy it, but to see what is wrong and to fume about it. And this is exactly why the partner-tyrant came to the bridge club to play.

There is nothing more corrosive to pleasant, happy bridge than one of these rotten apples. You can be playing with two other players who are jollity and joy personified, but if there is a single tyrant in the group, the whole game will take its character from him. And his partner's life will be undiluted misery.

Such tyranny does more harm than ignorance, inaccuracy, and poor holding combined, because it commits a partnership to the precise antithesis of what it needs: confidence in each other, warmth and camaraderie, all adding up to a relaxed relationship in which mental effort can flourish. The tyranny may take many forms, the most obvious of which is the diatribe:

"Now what in hell did you respond with, partner? I mean, you had nothing! If I'd have opened half a spade, you couldn't have responded three quarters of a no trump! And I gave you a shutout bid. Don't you know what a sign-off is? Don't you ever *read* anything about bridge?"

P. Hal Sims was a particularly overbearing partner, and this was probably his only drawback as a bridge player. Once a lady asked him how she had played her cards. "Like a millionaire," said Sims. When another partner asked how he should have played his hand, Sims cracked: "Under an assumed name!"

But Sims at least had the intellectual resources to make up for the discomfort his sharp tongue sometimes gave his partners. The average garden-variety tyrant has no such resources; he merely has read one more chapter than his partner, or has played a bit longer, or simply has a loud voice combined with poor manners, a dubious parlay.

The most common result of this partner-tyranny is underbidding, and for a number of reasons. Mostly it just seems safer to underbid with a tyrant, even though underbidding is expensive mathematically. You arrive at a contract of three spades, and you make four easily. Partner-tyrant may be annoyed, but usually he will restrain himself because, after all, 90 points are being chalked up below the line, and his team has made *something*. But if you bid four spades and make three, partner is now incensed because the opponents are getting 50 or 100 or 200 points. Now he says, "Why in the world did you take us so high?"

Hence a tendency to underbid; it protects us from such a typically tyrannical partner. The fact that the partner is showing obtuseness in elementary arithmetic has nothing to do with the matter. Most of us would rather appease idiocy than risk its loud scorn. A simple look at the two hands we've been talking about will show the mathematical realities ignored by partner-tyrant. When we bid three spades and made four, we scored 90 below and 30 above but missed scoring a game, a leg on a rubber, or even a 700 rubber. The loss, through underbidding, was something between 300 and 700 points. But partner-tyrant was silent. In the second case, when we bid four and made three and partner blew his top, we risked a penalty of 50 to 100 points in order to have a crack at 300 to 700 points. The odds were roughly six to one in our favor, and we'd have been crazy not to take them. As is so often the case with tyrants, this one was annoyed when he should have been pleased and pleased when he should have been annoyed.

I have a friend who has been playing contract bridge for about three hours less than Harold Vanderbilt (who invented the game) and still makes the same errors. My friend is positively immune to bridge; on occasion, he can even be counted on to forget the score, a mistake that should not be made by players above the age of six.

And yet I get along very well with this player. We have scored many a top in duplicate competition, won some tournaments, and now and then picked up some coin of the realm in rubber bridge. This is because I jolly him along; I tell him how much he has improved; I rave and fuss over him when he makes one of his rare (and often accidental) good plays. I pride myself on getting 105 per cent out of him.

But what happens when he cuts a tyrant in a rubber bridge game? At the first insult from the other side of the table, my friend folds up. He overbids and underbids, leads the opponents' strong suit, and fails to see any and all signals. And the rude tyrant who drew him gets just what he deserved: a poor result.

I confess there is no simple solution for handling the tyrant. My own approach (which I confess doesn't always work) is to agree with just about everything he says. "You're quite right, partner," I'll say. "If I'd seen the other hands, I would have done what you suggest. But you're absolutely right. I made a bad bid." Often this will shut them up. If you say you're wrong, it seems to satisfy some primordial craving in them, and they let up on you.

It isn't often that I have to face the problem of the bullying partner now; so perhaps I'm not so skilled at handling him as I once imagined I was. In the long run, I was luckier than most; my game reached a level where it was difficult to treat me rudely. But even today, after decades of building a reputation I still occasionally cut myself a partner who tries to explain the finer points of the game to me. Not that there aren't plenty of finer points for all of us to learn. But I am sometimes "corrected" by run-of-the-mill club players whose first master point won't come in until the next mail, if indeed it will ever come in. It's not so easy to be philosophical then.

But be careful! The teaching compulsion is bad bridge, bad manners, and bad economy. And the next time some pompous pedant tries to teach you a lesson at the bridge table, r'ar back and tell him:

"Teacher, teach thyself! And furthermore, in the words of Dorothy Dix . . ."

This is not rudeness. It is self-preservation.

Three rules of the road

Most top bridge players define a "mistake" as any bid or play they wouldn't make. I don't share this lofty attitude, but I do have strong personal feelings on the subject of table tactics and table manners. It just seems to me that there are certain things one *doesn't* do at the bridge table, whether they are violations of the laws of contract bridge or not. Some of these errors will merely cost you points; others will cost you friends.

Perhaps my most extreme personal prejudice is against excessive drinking at the bridge table. It's difficult to take any sort of position against alcohol without appearing to be a prig; so let me emphasize that some of my best friends are two-fisted drinkers, and I don't mind an occasional nip myself. Drinking can be good fun, and bridge can be good fun, but the two together produce neither good fun nor good bridge. How could it be otherwise? Whatever one can say in behalf of alcohol, it is not known for its salutary effect on one's judgment. And bridge is, first and foremost, a game of judgment. To say that alcohol enlivens a bridge game is to say that tying Gordie Howe's skates together enlivens his hockey game.

I also have a prejudice against excessive conversation during the play of a hand, although it is usually money in the bank for me. Constant chitter-chatter has the effect of distracting most players, but for some reason it has hardly any effect on my concentration. I slip off into a silent world of my own, consisting of fifty-two cards and certain probabilities, and all the talk in the world can't reach me. But for the average player, talk is deadly; it disrupts his concentration, and it changes the nature of the game. Opponents who talk through the playing of a slam, for example, will make you rich if you can find enough of them. They will almost always talk themselves out of making the hand. Why? You, as defender, usually have a lot less to remember than the declarer; you only have one or two cards with any potential for trick-taking. But declarer has to make all his cards good, or all but one. He is the one who needs silence, and he is the one who all too often doesn't provide it for himself.

After a hand has been played, it is often rewarding to talk about it, but the habit of the galloping post mortem can be overdone. My personal opinion is that a prolonged post mortem is rude unless it is clearly of interest to all four players. These two-man shouting matches between partners, with the opponents sitting embarrassedly by, are *de trop*.

Most such discourtesies could be avoided if players would remember that bridge is not only a partnership game, as everybody keeps saying, but a game for four. The opponents are not on the premises solely for the sake of providing you and your partner with an enchanted evening; they are also there to play, to have some good times of their own, and so you should get on with it. I frown on such dilly-dallying antics as automatically exchanging hands with partner as soon as you have won the auction, so that each of you can sit there and nod knowingly while the poor opponents, who are understandably eager to play the hand and get on to the next, are expected to wait patiently until the mutual inspection is over. The thing to remember is that the opponents can't slide their cards across the table and ruminate on each other's bidding; so there's no reason why you should do it.

Table tactics of a game for four

I used to belong to a bridge club where this habit was ended thoroughly and completely, courtesy of one angry player to whom it was anathema. Whenever an opponent slid his cards across the table, this fellow would intercept the hand and fan it.

"Oh, I'm sorry," he would say. "I just saw that hand out there in the middle of the table, and I automatically reached for it."

When an opponent became angry and demand penalties, this man would fix him with a frigid stare and intone with majestic dignity: "And under what section of the rules of contract bridge do you claim your penalties?" There was no answer to that one, of course; nothing in the rules of the game prevents you from grabbing a slapped-down hand, flinging it into the fire, or exchanging it for your own. Players should keep their hands in hand; they ignore this at their own risk.

When everything depends on the anonymity of your hand

You can chalk all the foregoing up to an eldering bridge player's personal crotchetiness, if you wish. Your game won't suffer—at least, it won't suffer much—if you choose to disregard my personal rules of the road. But now let's look at some table tactics that can cost you points and plenty of them. For a starter, consider the way you sort your cards:

You didn't think it mattered? Well, it shouldn't, but it does. Every now and then you will run into a sharpie who watches very closely how you sort, and if you're not paying attention, he will soon be able to spot singletons, voids, lengths of suits and other valuable tidbits of information about your hand. (These sharpies are never consistent winners; their minds are too full of tricks and too empty of solid bridge knowledge. But they can take you for a short, expensive ride if you don't know how to counter them.)

The average player sorts his cards from left to right in descending order, like this:

Now consider what you are telling a crafty opponent if this method of sorting becomes a pattern with you. He knows that the card on the far right is the lowest of its suit. Conversely, he knows that your far left card is the highest of its suit. And see what happens if your hand is shaped like this:

As soon as you play the deuce of spades from the left end of your hand, opponents know you are out of spades. (If the deuce is your highest, you can't have any more.) As soon as you play the ace of clubs from the right side of your hand, they know you're out of clubs. (If the ace is your lowest, you can't have any more.) These are oversimplified examples, but not at all far-fetched. The left-hand card doesn't have to be a deuce to give your hand away. Suppose it is a six, but one of the opponents, seeing his own hand and dummy, can account for the five, four, three, and two; then he knows you are leading a singleton. There are all sorts of variations on these possibilities, and a simple, straightforward way out of them: Don't sort your hand in a pattern. And above all, never put singletons and doubletons on either end of your hand. It is also unsound to line up your trumps at the far right, as many players do. I am guilty of that myself, but only for the edification of kibitzers, a much maligned breed whom I like to encourage. Until you have a posse of kibitzers trailing you, you'd do well to mix up your sorting, and no one will be able to read the anonymous backs of your cards.

The case of the missing card

I don't suppose it is necessary to advise you to take care that you get all your suits together and don't mix your diamonds with your hearts, etc., or is it? A list of star players who have committed this classic blunder would read like a Who's Who of Bridge, and conspicuous on the list would be the name of yours truly. Stories about my own misplacing of cards are too painful for me to recount, so I will tell you about a hand that was played in Reading, Pennsylvania, where my old friend Dr. Leon Altman heard his partner open with a bid of two no trump. "Doc" had enough points in his hand to jump to four no trump, but he raised the contract to a modest three no trump, which was immediately doubled and redoubled. Doc's partner went down 1600 points and explained: "I'm sorry, I had a card misplaced."

Doc asked innocently: "Only one card?"

In a tournament, I sat East with another old friend, Percy "Shorty" Sheardown of Toronto, as my partner, when this hand came up:

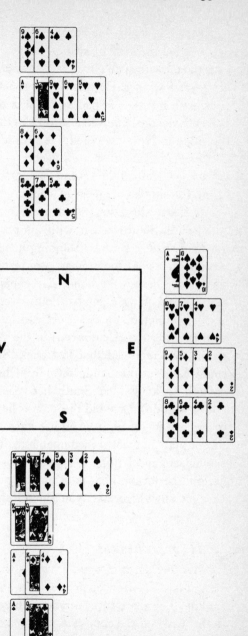

South was declarer at six spades. Shorty opened the queen of diamonds, which South won in his hand. Then declarer led the king of spades, keeping his hand hovering over the table in such a manner as to leave no doubt that his king was a winner. He was visibly shocked when I took the trick with my ace of spades. He peered into his own hand and conspicuously moved a card from the end of the hand to the middle. Now everybody at the table knew what had happened: he had misplaced the ace of clubs at the head of his spades. He had thought he had seven spades to the A K Q, and a singleton queen of clubs.

No better lead suggested itself to me, so I led back a small club. South took it with his ace and laid down the queen of spades. Both outstanding honors dropped, and the slam became a laydown. Shorty said later, "Sorry, Charlie, I could have beaten the hand." He explained that he should have led the king of clubs. South would have played his queen "singleton" on the trick, and by the time he discovered that his ace of clubs was in the wrong pew, he could never have regained that lost trick. Shorty was right; he could have set the hand, but only if he'd been clairvoyant enough to know that South had mis-sorted. Sadder yet, South wouldn't have bid the slam if he had sorted his hand properly and certainly wouldn't have taken the successful line of play that was forced upon him. There's a moral there someplace, and I think it is as follows: when you can't be careful, be lucky. That is as good a piece of advice as you can get anywhere, and you should cherish it.

He who hesitates . . .

Another piece of good advice is to avoid the prolonged hesitation, the trance, or, as it is sometimes called, the huddle. There are several types. There is the trance aimed at throwing off the opponent, as, for example, when a player holds a singleton and wants opponent to think that he has more than one. This is downright shady, and is grounds for expulsion from most clubs, as well it should be. There is a second type of huddle where the player is trying to figure out, or "count," the hand. For a reasonable length of time, this trance is perfectly permissible. On important plays like the opening lead, it is even recommended. But after that reasonable length of time is over, I say play a card, even if it's the wrong one. Nothing at a bridge table is so important that every other player should be forced to sit in ennui while a great thinker thinks.

But the worst trance is the informative one, a fraternity brother of the double that tells declarer where the outstanding honors are. The informative, or Western Union, trance comes up most frequently when the player to your right is finessing against you, and you have the finessable card, and you're trying to figure out whether to play it or duck. By the time you have hesitated, it makes no difference: declarer knows where the card is and can play accordingly. But if the declarer leads through your king-deuce to an ace-queen on the board, why should you spend five minutes puzzling over your play? You should have known the instant the dummy went down that this was going to happen, and you should already have decided whether to cover or duck. If you now play crisply and unhesitatingly, the declarer at least has been given the opportunity to make the wrong play by coming up with the ace in a fit of panic. A poor play on his part? Of course. But you've at least given him a chance to commit an error, and every now and then some obliging declarer will take you up on it.

At a bare minimum, you should be able to play your cards one trick in advance, whether you have that mysterious quality known as card sense or not and whether you have as bad a memory as mine or not. You should have a general idea of what you're going to do when it finally comes around to, say, that ticklish ace-queen of hearts on the board, and you should have some idea whether you're going to lead up to that king of spades in your hand or lay a trap for the opponents to lead up to it. These may be general guidelines in your head, but specifically you should always be one trick ahead of yourself. When you take a trick, you should have a definite idea of what you are going to lead next. And during the development of that trick, you're figuring out what to do on the following one. If I can do this with my inadequate memory, anybody can.

But not everybody thinks ahead. Consider how many times you've seen a player begin a finesse by leading low from his own hand. Next-hand plays low, and now declarer goes into a long trance trying to figure out whether to go through with the finesse or play his ace on the board. This is outrageous, and should call for a five-yard penalty for delaying the game. When this player started his finesse, he knew there were two possibilities to his left: the player would either come up with the queen, or he wouldn't. So why should the finesser be completely taken aback now that one of those two eventualities has come to pass? But all too frequently he is, thus marking himself as the type of player who can't plan one trick ahead, or even one card ahead. He has led low from his hand with a single idea: that it will force the queen immediately, and his finesse will be an instant success. What if it isn't? He hasn't figured that out yet. This is not bridge; it is roulette, or craps, or ticktack-toe; anything but bridge.

The only glimmer of brightness in the picture is that you will not need any advice on how to win from this hapless fellow. Just follow suit and don't revoke, and the rest will take care of itself, especially the money.

The rapid-fire man

There is one type of player who all but demands coun-terattack. At times only an artificial trance of your own will handle the character I call the "speeder." Like most speed-ers, he knows he's being naughty, but he pretends that it's all in the game. This is the player who takes his time about figuring his line of play; then, once having figured it, pounds his leads down on the table with assembly-line rapidity, hoping to dazzle you with his skill. He seeks to give the impression that it's ridiculous to try to defend against this contract; it's practically a laydown; but if you have to defend against it, let's get the boring thing over as quickly as possible. And down come his leads one after another, while his hand lingers over the center of the table, waiting to play his next winner.

The best way to treat the speeder is to sit back in your chair, look at your cards, light a cigarette, study your cards a bit more, puff on your cigarette contemplatively, ask the hostess for another cup of coffee, inspect your cards once again, and finally play that four of clubs you were intending to play from the beginning. Now of course you can't do this with a singleton, or if the effect of your hesitation would be to clearly misplace a finessable honor. That would be coffee-housing, and I am not recommending coffeehousing as a solution to anything. But when you can make an ethical pause and break up a speeder's rhythm, by all means do it. Most of the time a speeder is trying, consciously or otherwise, to get away with something, and he figures the best way is to rush you into an error. That's all the more reason for you to take your time and think. Be especially watchful when he has set up a string of cards and is running it. He'll have the next card in his hand ready to play before the trick is even finished. But the end result of a long run of cards is often a squeeze. When you're a potential squeezee, you need all the clear thinking you can muster, and that means taking some time to ponder, even on the most "automatic" discards.

The speeder is often the type of player who, in his boyish exuberance, grabs the trick and throws it on his pile before you've had a chance to see what has fallen. Some will go so far as to cover up their own card with their hand and rake in the other three cards simultaneously. This sort of player is trying to tell you, "I'm just discarding junk from my hand, the same as you are." But when a squeeze is shaping up, it becomes all the more important to see what small card declarer is discarding. When a speeder tries this maneuver on me, I simply demand to see the whole trick, card by card, and on the next trick I make the same demand. After this has happened a few times, he's lost more time by my demands than he's gained by his own sleight-of-hand, and he cuts it out, which is what I wanted him to do in the first place.

A second cousin once removed of the speeder is the player who pulls out his card before it's his turn to play, as though to announce: "My play is automatic; I've got to play this card no matter what the rest of you play." This can be highly unethical, as when the player sitting there waving his "automatic" is actually getting ready to over-ruff, or when he's holding a finessable card. And when the play isn't unethical, it's revealing. The opponent may be trying to guess which way to finesse until such a kindly player shows him the way by flashing his "automatic" card. If I told you the names of some of the international champions who consistently make this basic error in table tactics, you would not believe me, and I would be hard-pressed to explain how they became champions in the first place.

Reflections on a lifetime

Every so often in my meanderings around the globe, I run into someone who says, in effect: "Mr. Goren, I know you make your living from bridge, but tell me: Do you still enjoy playing the game?" I always answer them with this story:

An Irishman told his wife to awaken him whenever he wanted a whisky. "And how am I to know when you're thirsty?" asked his wife.

"Don't worry," he answered. "Whenever you wake me, I'll be thirsty!"

Well, whenever you wake me, I'll be ready to play bridge: rubber bridge, duplicate, Chicago, bridge-for-two, or even that crazy new three-handed game where the dealer is automatically declarer at two no trump doubled. If it's bridge, please deal me in.

I happen to be a sports fanatic; there is hardly a bowl game, a Stanley Cup playoff, a world-series game, or a championship fight that I haven't seen either in the flesh or parked in front of my faithful television set. But the biggest thrill for me remains the same as it was thirty years ago: to walk into a pleasant apartment with congenial companions and sit down to an evening of bridge. I enshroud myself in the bridge mystique: the soft lighting that shines just right on your 150 honors; the sharpened pencils for marking down your redoubled slams; the square yard of felt that gives a little when you bang down your aces and stagger the opposition with your *mot juste:* "Not through the Iron Duke!" You may think I'm overemphatic about the accoutrements of the game, but to me the atmosphere is almost as important as the cards. I've noticed that Helen Sobel and I don't play at our best when we're mired in some dingy corner with poor lighting and tobacco smoke you can slice, and many other tournament players are equally sensitive. I once knew a man who developed mysterious head-aches every Tuesday morning. A doctor who was years ahead of his time worked out the diagnosis by the process of elimination. My friend played bridge in the same club on the same brown felt table top every Monday night, and he was allergic to this particular shade of brown. Myself, I'm allergic to dreary surroundings.

Not that I haven't had to make the best of a few bizarre settings. I remember a weekend when three classmates and I hitchhiked from McGill University, in Montreal, to Syracuse, New York, a distance of about three hundred miles. We were picked up by a potato truck, and hardly had the driver gone a hundred yards before we had improvised a table out of potato sacks, chosen sides, and started a bridge game that lasted for ten rocking, hectic, drafty, and altogether enjoyable hours. And not for money either. This was in a period when I thought a cue bid was an invitation to shoot pool; that's how advanced my game was.

I suppose a goodly portion of the charm of bridge is in your companions, your fellow aficionados of the game. I've always found that the bridge player is more interesting than the average person, and it stands to reason. All other things being equal, the person who does some thinking, who accepts some sort of intellectual challenge, is bound to be more scintillating than the drone who orders his life by the numbers. I can look back on thousands of happy hours spent in the company of bridge players, both at the table and away from it. For one thing, bridge players seem to have more fun than humans. Jokes, practical and otherwise, play a big role in their lives—don't ask me why. Certain of my tournament-circuit friends deal almost entirely in punch lines. One of them will say, "Yeh, but what's the first prize?" or "How do you start a flood?" or "I gave at the office," and the others will break up with the memory of the whole joke. There's no point in telling entire jokes to bridge players; the punch line will usually suffice. Would you go so far as to say that bridge players in the mass are perhaps candidates for what Jonathan Winters calls "the funny farm?" Well, you may be right, but look at the fun we have, even at our own expense. I remember a player who came reeling away from the table, a handkerchief pressed against his mouth so his laughter wouldn't disturb the other players. What was so funny? I asked him. He told me that his partner had just gone down 1400 points at three no trump, and after taking this horrendous beating, the partner had said in total seriousness: "If they'd led clubs, they'd have killed me!"

I can remember long conferences over which way the cards were running that night, and certain players who would not sit down to the table until they checked the bathtub for the proper direction of card-flow, proving that bridge is not immune to the superstitions that beset other sports. And I can remember the most serious discussions over minutiae, like the man who made a formal complaint at the Cavendish Club because Harold Ogust's dachshund, Silky, the only canine ever to be permitted on those hallowed premises, was looking at his hand. Mind you, this member did not object to Silky's presence in the club. But he did not want her peering into his hand! Now when you've spent your life with people like that, how are you going to find time to be bored?

I remember so many people who all but lived for bridge, who would almost have curled up and withered away if they hadn't been able to play. Most of them found it difficult even to express themselves in non-bridge terms away from the table. There was a young man who introduced himself to me and said he was from Sulligent, Alabama.

"Sulligent, Alabama?" I said. "How big is Sulligent?"

"Oh," he said, "about four tables."

And I remember a man who was playing in a tournament far from home when he received word that his wife had died. The next available train was six hours later, and if you don't know what that man did for the next six hours, then you don't know bridge players. (You're right, and he never played better.)

I wasn't any different. For years I've been getting a perverse joy out of circulating the story that I wasn't doing very well as a Philadelphia lawyer and so turned to bridge in desperation, but the truth is that I was doing quite nicely in law when I simply decided to throw it all in. The law, fraught as it was with everything from petty claims to murder, didn't seem as interesting to me as the endless permutations and combinations involved in fifty-two cards and four players. And when I found that I seemed to have a natural flair for bridge, I decided to make it my life. None of this happened overnight, however. I suppose the late Woolcott Roberts should get a lot of the credit—or blame. Roberts, an All-American football player at Navy in 1919, began coming to our bridge club in Philadelphia in the late 1920s and immediately showed everybody that he had a savvy for the game. I was playing reasonably well myself, and I went to him and said, "Woolk, what's the sense of beating our brains out against each other? Let's team up." We did, and for two years we found it all but impossible to lose a match. Somebody organized a monthly duplicate tournament, and in seven of the first eight months, the Roberts-Goren pair was first; one tournament got away from us by a half point. Woolcott Roberts was the best unschooled bridge player I have ever seen. In minutes, he worked out plays that I would have to study for days to understand, plays that now take up whole chapters in text books. The only person who ever came close to him for natural bridge moxie is Helen Sobel.

It was about 1928 when contract replaced auction bridge, and I discovered I could make the transition with hardly any trouble, certainly with less trouble than most of my competitors. To put it bluntly, immodestly, and factually, I almost never lost in those years. If I didn't win a match, I almost felt I had been cheated. When I entered a tournament, it was with the full expectation of winning; I couldn't see any other possibility, and usually I was right. I was the way Sandy Koufax is nowadays; when he gives up a hit, it's unusual, and when he gives up a run, it's news.

So I was a winner, and if there's anything more fun than playing at bridge, it is winning at bridge. That's one of the reasons I never became enamored of playing bridge for money. The game was already so much fun; money could add nothing to it. There was such richness and variety and tang; there was so much challenge and so many different situations to be mastered. It wasn't like poker, where the way you managed your money was far more important than the way you managed your cards. At the beginning of my bridge career, I played in the clubs for about a quarter of a cent a point, never more, and I wouldn't have played for this much except that I couldn't get a good game otherwise. Each week I would win thirty or forty dollars at a quarter of a cent, and after a while it almost seemed like cheating to me. That's why I am not impressed today by certain bridge experts who have reputations for being big sports because they are always willing to challenge club players for high stakes. I don't think these experts should be allowed to play for high stakes, because *they can't lose*, at least not for longer than a few rubbers. And neither can I

Once, in St. Louis, I did find myself in a dollar-a-point game, but only in the sense that a horse finds himself in a $100,000-stakes race; the horse isn't putting up any money, nor was I. My partner, a wealthy stockbroker, was betting our opponents one dollar a point. And wouldn't you know it—on the very first hand I made a Little League error on defense and gave the opponents a game (worth three hundred to four hundred dollars). I could have soaked my head in the Mississippi. But my partner never blinked, and so I took a leaf from the children's books and the television serials and buckled down to the task at hand. We won handily.

The most arduous session I've ever been in began one night at the Wissahickon Bridge Club in Philadelphia, where I ran afoul of three of the youngest old men in the game. Charlie Warner was in his late sixties; Dr. Shelley was only a few years younger, and Dr. Kirkbride was the baby of the trio at fifty-six. They inveigled me into a game that started at eight o'clock on a Friday night. At 2 A.M., an hour when all good bridge players should be sound asleep, this unholy trio suggested that we send out for coffee and sandwiches and play till dawn. We played till dawn and right on into Saturday night, when we sent out for sandwiches and coffee once more. When Sunday's morning sun came up, and my head began to droop, my cronies gave me a verbal pasting for being "too old for this game." (I was thirty.) So I played on until spades began to look like clubs. Late Sunday night, after more than forty-eight hours at the table, I corked off right in the middle of a hand, and no amount of shaking or prodding by those bulldogs could wake me up. I never heard the end of that.

But if the two good doctors and Charlie Warner were still around and wanted to have a go at it again, they could count me in. Come to think of it, there's very little I would do differently if I had another crack at life, and certainly I wouldn't miss that two-day session at the munificent stakes of a tenth of a cent a point. Or any other session with companionable players. When it comes to the noble game of bridge, I feel much the same as Talleyrand felt about the noble game of whist. The French statesman invited a man to make a fourth at whist, whereupon the flustered visitor had to admit that he didn't know the game. "Young man!" said a shocked Talleyrand. "You do not play whist? What a sad old age you reserve for yourself!"

The Quizzes

70 tests of lessons learned

Quiz 1

You are South. What action do you take on each of the following hands?

1. You hold:

    ♠ Q J 9 7 3   ♥ 3   ♦ J 10 9 6 4   ♣ 5 2

    The bidding has proceeded:

SOUTH	WEST	NORTH	EAST
Pass	1 ♥	Double	2 ♥
?			

2. As South you hold:

    ♠ A K 9 6 5   ♥ 3 2   ♦ A K 6 4   ♣ K 8

    The bidding has proceeded:

SOUTH	NORTH
1 ♠	3 ♠
?	

3. As South you hold:

    ♠ A J 9 6 5   ♥ K 9   ♦ A 7 3   ♣ K J 4

    You are the dealer. What is your opening bid?

4. As South you hold:

    ♠ 9 4   ♥ A J 10 3   ♦ A 8 2   ♣ A K 9 7

    You are the dealer. What is your opening bid?

155

5. As South you hold:

   ♠ 3 ♥ A K 10 6 4 ♦ 3 2 ♣ A Q 10 9 5

   The bidding has proceeded:

SOUTH	NORTH
1 ♥	1 ♠
2 ♣	2 ♠
?	

6. As South you hold:

   ♠ 3 ♥ A 6 4 ♦ K Q 10 4 2 ♣ A J 10 3

   The bidding has proceeded:

NORTH	SOUTH
1 ♠	2 ♦
2 ♥	?

7. As South you hold:

   ♠ 10 9 4 3 ♥ A K 3 ♦ J 6 2 ♣ 9 8 6

   The bidding has proceeded:

NORTH	EAST	SOUTH
1 NT	2 ♠	?

8. As South you hold:

   ♠ K 9 7 5 ♥ A 3 ♦ A 7 6 5 ♣ 4 3 2

   The bidding has proceeded:

NORTH	EAST	SOUTH
1 ♠	3 ♥	?

   (pre-emptive)

9. As South you hold:

   ♠ A 10 8 ♥ K 8 6 4 3 ♦ None ♣ J 9 7 6 2

   The bidding has proceeded:

NORTH	EAST	SOUTH	WEST
1 ♦	1 ♠	Pass	2 ♠
Double	Pass	?	

10. As South you hold:

♠ A K Q 6 4 3   ♥ None   ♦ Q J 10 2   ♣ 6 4 3

The bidding has proceeded:

SOUTH	WEST	NORTH	EAST
1 ♠	2 ♥	Double	Pass
?			

Quiz 1–ANSWERS

1. *Two Spades.*   Partner has announced an interest in spades by virtue of his takeout double of one heart, and you should seize this opportunity to compete. While you have but four points in high cards, your excellent distribution more than compensates for your lack of points. When you hold a 5–5–2–1 distribution it is safe to bid twice as much as is warranted by your actual point count.

2. *Four Diamonds.*   Partner has shown the equal of an opening bid by his jump raise, which shows a point count of 13 to 16 in support of your suit. Your hand is worth 20, so that the combined assets of the partnership place you in the slam zone. The only thing that might defeat a slam is the lack of controls. A four-diamond bid by you announces a slam interest and asks partner to show his controls by means of cue bids if his hand warrants such action. If partner shows the ace of hearts, you will bid the slam directly. If partner responds with five clubs, you can re-cue bid your diamonds. Partner may have a singleton heart, and a slam will still have an excellent play.

3. *One No Trump.*   You have a total of 16 high-card points, and the possession of a five-card major suit should not deter you from precisely limiting your hand by a bid of one no trump. The argument against the opening bid of one spade is that you will be in somewhat of a quandary if partner responds with one no trump. If you then decide to pass, you may well miss a game. On the other hand, if you elect to raise to two no trump, you may be beyond your means. The initial opening bid of one no trump solves this possible dilemma and also guards your tenace positions against attack from the opening lead.

4. *One Heart.* **Though the hand counts 16 points and is balanced, it is not our practice to open the bidding with one no trump when we hold a worthless doubleton in one of the suits. If partner responds with one spade, it is our intention to show the club suit. If he rebids two diamonds, thereby denoting a hand which is average or better in strength, the hand is good enough to raise him to the three level. Observe that it would be poor policy to rebid one no trump after a one-spade response. Such a call would show a maximum of 15 high-card points. The hand is a shade or so better than that.**

5. *Pass.* **Partner's refusal to take a preference in one of your suits makes the possibilities of game all but remote. When a misfit becomes apparent, it behooves the partner who holds the high cards to subordinate his desires to his partner's will. The high-card winners will be useful in a spade contract. Partner's spades are not likely to prove a balm in a diamond or heart contract.**

6. *Three Clubs.* **We recognize that we have the ingredients for a game contract and offer three clubs as the bid that gives us the widest latitude in reaching the best possible contract. If partner rebids his hearts, we can raise to game in that suit. If he bids three diamonds, a belated heart preference will make it clear that you do not have four-card support in that suit, for surely you would have preferred to raise him directly. If partner rebids three no trump, such a contract will not be distasteful. A direct leap to three no trump leaves us cold. Such a drastic action might lead to an inferior contract and precludes the possibility of reaching a slam, which is by no means out of the question at this point.**

7. *Double.* **Partner can be expected to produce four winners by virtue of his one no-trump opening and you have three (the possession of four trumps is regarded as one winner for defensive purposes) so that a minimum of 300 points in penalties is in sight. It would be inadvisable to bid two no trump, for game is far from a certainty whereas the prospects of a windfall appear bright. Furthermore, if partner had the ingredients to carry on to game after a raise by you, they would only serve to sweeten the kitty in a contract of two spades doubled.**

8. *Four Spades.* **You have the equal of an opening bid in support of spades and are obliged to take drastic action, inasmuch as the enemy activity has deprived you of valuable bidding space. It would be a distinct error to bid but three spades, for such a**

call is not forcing and partner may not be able to carry on. If a slam is lurking in the shadows, partner is still at liberty to bid, since your jump raise has announced a hand of opening-bid strength.

9. *Three Spades.* Partner has shown splendid support for the remaining suits, since he has forced you to compete at the level of three by means of his double of two spades. Since you have virtually the equal of an opening bid in support of clubs or hearts, you should apprise partner of your values by means of a cue bid. If partner bids four hearts, you will pass. If he shows the club suit, you intend, of course, to bid on to game in that suit.

10. *Two Spades.* Partner has offered you the proposition of considering the advisability of playing a contract of two hearts doubled. Since your hand is lacking in defensive strength, it will probably be a disappointment to him, and you should indicate this by bidding two spades. If partner proceeds in spite of your warning, you should fully expect to make a game.

1. As South you hold:

♠ Q J 10 9 8 3 2   ♥ A Q 3   ♦ 7   ♣ 10 9

What is your opening bid?

2. With East-West vulnerable, as South you hold:

♠ 10 9 7 6 5 3 2   ♥ 9 8 6 5   ♦ 3   ♣ 9

The bidding has proceeded:

WEST	NORTH	EAST	SOUTH
1 ♥	Pass	2 ♦	Pass
3 ♥	Pass	4 ♥	Pass
4 ♠	Double	5 ♣	Pass
5 ♦	Pass	6 ♥	?

What do you bid now?

3. As South you hold:

♠ Q J 10 9 5   ♥ None   ♦ A K Q 6 3 2   ♣ 3 2

The bidding has proceeded:

NORTH	EAST	SOUTH
1 ♠	Pass	?

What do you bid now?

4. As South you hold:

♠ 10 3 2   ♥ K 9 5   ♦ A Q 10 9 4   ♣ A K

The bidding has proceeded:

SOUTH	NORTH
1 NT	2 NT
?	

What do you bid now?

5. As South you hold:

♠ 2   ♥ A Q 9   ♦ J 10 7 3 2   ♣ Q 10 9 2

The bidding has proceeded:

EAST	SOUTH	WEST	NORTH
1 ♦	Pass	Pass	2 ♦
Pass	3 ♣	Pass	3 ♥
Pass	?		

What do you bid now?

6. As South and with both sides vulnerable, you hold:

♠ 10 3 2   ♥ A K   ♦ A 10 9 6 5   ♣ A Q 3

The bidding has proceeded:

EAST	SOUTH	WEST	NORTH
1 ♠	Double	2 ♠	3 ♦
3 ♥	?		

What do you bid now?

7. As South you hold:

♠ K Q 5 4 3   ♥ A K J 3 2   ♦ Q 3   ♣ 2

The bidding has proceeded:

SOUTH	NORTH
1 ♠	2 ♠
?	

What do you bid now?

8. As South you hold:

    ♠ K 5   ♥ 10 9 2   ♦ A   ♣ A K Q J 4 3 2

    The bidding has proceeded:

EAST	SOUTH
1 ♠	?

    What do you bid now?

9. North-South are vulnerable. You as South hold:

    ♠ None   ♥ A 10 9 7 5   ♦ A 3   ♣ A K 8 7 6 3

    The bidding has proceeded:

SOUTH	WEST	NORTH	EAST
1 ♣	1 ♠	2 ♥	3 ♠
?			

    What do you bid now?

10. As South you hold:

    ♠ 2   ♥ A 9 7 3   ♦ A J 10 9 5   ♣ Q J 3

    The bidding has proceeded:

SOUTH	WEST	NORTH	EAST
1 ♦	Double	2 ♦	Pass
?			

    What do you bid now?

Quiz **2**–ANSWERS

1. *Pass.* At first glance, it appears that an opening pre-emptive call of three spades would be desirable, but that would convey the impression that your hand was virtually defenseless. A pre-emptive opening should be reserved for those hands in which the majority of the high-card strength is concentrated in the bid suit. It is wiser to pass first and back into the bidding later if the enemy do not display signs of excess strength.

2. *Six Spades.* The propaganda of the enemy has disclosed that your side has an abundance of spades and also that partner has at most a singleton in the heart suit. Since you have singletons in both of the minor suits, it should become apparent that a sacrifice bid will not prove too costly. Actually, it would cost but 100 points. (Partner's hand was as follows):

♠ A Q J 8 4   ♥ None   ♦ 7 5 2   ♣ Q J 10 8 3

It should be observed that a sacrifice bid of seven spades does not cost too much of a premium if the opposition persists to the grand slam.

3. *Six Spades.* There is no point in fishing around for a grand slam on this hand, for you are not at all certain that a small slam is a sure thing. Launching into a Blackwood inquiry may provide the opposition with the opportunity to call in clubs, an action which may prove to be disastrous to your cause. All things considered, the blasting bid of six spades keeps everything in the dark, and may elicit a favorable opening lead.

4. *Three No Trump.* While you hold a minimum hand in high-card strength, the possession of a good five-card suit and two extra tens should sway you into proceeding. Remember the rewards for making a game more than compensate for the times which you are set a trick or two. In most cases, a game should be contracted for when there is a reasonable chance that it is makable.

5. *Five Hearts.* Partner has insisted that a game be reached even though your hand could have been "pointless." Since you have splendid support and a singleton in the other suit in which partner has announced an interest, it behooves you to take positive action. A call of four hearts would merely be fulfilling the obligation forced upon you by partner. On the other hand, five hearts displays an intense interest in slam and leaves it up to partner to make the final decision.

6. *Six Diamonds.* With both opponents competing vulnerable, partner is marked with a singleton spade. If the slam is not laydown, it will subsequently be on at most a finesse in clubs which figures to be successful in view of the fact that East has opened the bidding and rebid three hearts without the tops in that suit. A call of five diamonds is acceptable but displays a reservist attitude. In any event, it places too much pressure on partner, for surely he will be unable to contract for a slam if he has two or three small hearts in his hand.

7. *Four Spades.* You have 18 points, and partner has shown between 7 and 10 points in support. If he has the right hand, a game bid is in order. Since there is no accurate method available for uncovering this fact, the direct approach is desirable. We definitely dislike the call of three hearts which will alert the opposition against a lead in that suit and may steer them into the correct defense. Another consideration against the three-heart call is that it conveys too much information to your adversaries, and might enable them to discover a successful sacrifice in one of the minor suits.

8. *Three No Trump.* It is far-fetched to envision slam possibilities after an adverse opening bid. As a matter of fact, game in clubs may be beyond reach, whereas a favorable opening lead will make a three no-trump contract laydown. Despite the fact that you have a wealth of high cards, your prospects for defeating a game in spades by the enemy are not too good. A bid of three no trump has the dual effect of disrupting their lines of communication as well as placing you in an advantageous position to score a game bonus.

9. *Four Hearts.* We agree you may be cold for six, or seven for that matter, but that is not the objective on this hand. Your main concern should be that of buying the contract at any level. Since the enemy are non-vulnerable, they will be only too happy to take a sacrifice if you suddenly leap to a slam, and you should be convinced that they have a good one. If you choose to travel slowly, and the opposition overbid you in turn, they might decide to let you play for a slam in the hopes that their competitive bidding has carried you overboard.

10. *Three Diamonds.* The question of whether you can make a game on this hand is not the issue at all, for partner's call has made it clear that your opponents have the better hand. However, if you pass two diamonds, you are furnishing them with a golden opportunity to find a spade fit, and prospects of defeating an adverse spade game are rather remote. Your call of three diamonds is considered an effort at muddying the waters in the hope that your left-hand opponent will find it inconvenient to compete at this high a level.

What is your action on the following?

1. As South you hold:

♠ Q J 10 9   ♥ K 8   ♦ 7 6 4   ♣ 9 4 3 2

The bidding has proceeded:

EAST	SOUTH	WEST	NORTH
1 ♠	Pass	1 NT	Pass
2 ♥	Pass	2 ♠	Pass
3 ♠	Pass	4 ♠	Pass
Pass	?		

2. As South you hold:

♠ 9 6 5   ♥ A K 10 9 4   ♦ 2   ♣ K Q 7 5

The bidding has proceeded:

SOUTH	WEST	NORTH	EAST
1 ♥	2 ♠	3 ♣	3 ♠
	(pre-emptive)		
4 ♣	Pass	4 ♥	4 ♠
5 ♥	5 ♠	Pass	Pass

3. As South you hold:

♠ 5 2   ♥ Q 10 9 4   ♦ A K 4   ♣ Q 10 9 3

The bidding has proceeded:

NORTH	EAST	SOUTH
1 ♠	2 ♥	?

4. As South you hold:

♠ 2　♥ A K 7 6 5　♦ Q J 10 9 4　♣ Q 3

The bidding has proceeded:

SOUTH	WEST	NORTH	EAST
1 ♥	1 ♠	Double	Pass
?			

5. As South you hold:

♠ J 9 8 6 5　♥ 6 3 2　♦ A 7 5　♣ A Q

The bidding has proceeded:

EAST	SOUTH	WEST	NORTH
1 ♠	Pass	3 ♥	Pass
4 ♥	Pass	5 ♦	Pass
5 ♥	Pass	6 ♥	Pass
Pass	?		

6. As South you hold:

♠ Q 7 5　♥ K Q J 10　♦ 3 2　♣ J 7 3 2

The bidding has proceeded:

EAST	SOUTH	WEST	NORTH
1 ♥	Pass	3 ♦	Pass
3 ♥	Pass	4 ♥	Pass
4 NT	Pass	5 ♥	Pass
6 ♥	?		

7. As South you hold:

♠ A Q J 6 3 2　♥ K 10 7 5　♦ Q 2　♣ 7

The bidding has proceeded:

SOUTH	NORTH
1 ♠	2 ♣
?	

8. As South you hold:

♠ Q 10 7 4   ♥ 2   ♦ K J 3   ♣ Q J 10 9 4

The bidding has proceeded:

WEST	NORTH	EAST	SOUTH
Pass	Pass	1 ♦	Pass
1 ♥	Pass	1 ♠	Pass
2 ♥	Pass	2 NT	Pass
3 NT	Pass	Pass	?

9. As South you hold:

♠ 4   ♥ A K Q 4   ♦ K 10 7 3   ♣ Q 6 4 2

The bidding has proceeded:

SOUTH	WEST	NORTH	EAST
1 ♥	Pass	3 ♥	3 ♠
?			

10. As South you hold:

♠ 9 8 7 6 5 4   ♥ 6 2   ♦ 4   ♣ 6 5 3 2

The bidding has proceeded:

WEST	NORTH	EAST	SOUTH
2 NT	Double	Pass	?

Quiz 3–ANSWERS

1. *Double.* The enemy activities have indicated that they do not have too much to spare, and your four good trumps should prove to be embarrassing. Moreover, partner may be able to supply two or three tricks to add to the mayhem, for the bidding has indicated that he is not without some values.

2. *Six Hearts.* Partner's pass of five spades is called a forcing pass and gives you the option of doubling the opposition or proceeding to six hearts. Since he is willing to contract for a slam, he cannot have more than one spade in his hand, and

also, he must have a very fine holding to offer you a choice. If partner held two or more spades, it would have been his duty to double the bid of five spades as a warning against proceeding to six hearts. There is a further consideration. Since your partnership holds hearts and clubs, it is not out of the realm of possibility that the opponents can make their contract of five spades. Whenever there is a serious doubt as whether to proceed or double, and the bidding has indicated that the hand is extremely distributional, the winning policy is to bid once more.

3. *Double.* Partner has opened the bidding and can be relied upon to produce three defensive winners. Your holding justifies the expectancy of winning four tricks as a minimum, thereby inflicting a 300-point or more setback. Curb your natural impulse to bid two no trump in such a situation, for if your side has a game, the corresponding yield from a double will exceed the value of the game. At times, a contract of three no trump will be defeated whereas the double of the adverse overcall will produce from 500 to 700 points.

4. *Two Diamonds.* We are not happy in removing partner's penalty double, but on examination of our hand, we feel that it is bound to be a disappointment to him defensively. If our side is to defeat a contract of one spade enough to compensate for our potential score (if we were to play the hand), we would, in effect be playing the hand in spades our way, and with our singleton, this would be far from tasteful to us. Since we would not be happy at all with this contract, we takeout to two diamonds.

5. *Pass.* While it seems highly probable that you will defeat the slam, it is poor mathematics to double. Surely you will not defeat the contract more than one trick, and you stand to gain but 50 points if you double. Moreover, the double of a slam calls for partner to make an abnormal lead (in this case, the lead of dummy's first suit, spades). If he complies, it is quite possible that you will fail to defeat the hand at all. On the other hand, if you remain silent, partner is bound to lead the unbid suit, and you will defeat the hand (if it can be defeated at all). It should be borne in mind that the opponents have contracted for a slam off two aces, and most likely one of them is void in a suit. A double on your part might steer them into making the deal—a swing of 1210 points in their favor. You are in effect willing to risk about 250 points to gain 50. We think that you are not a five-to-one favorite to beat the contract. For purposes of inspection, the complete deal follows:

```
                    NORTH
                    ♠ 4 3
                    ♥ 4
                    ♦ 9 8 6 4 3
                    ♣ 8 7 5 4 3
        WEST                        EAST
        ♠ K                         ♠ A Q 10 7 2
        ♥ A K Q J 10                ♥ 9 8 7 5
        ♦ K Q J 10 2                ♦ None
        ♣ 6 2                       ♣ K J 10 9
                    SOUTH
                    ♠ J 9 8 6 5
                    ♥ 6 3 2
                    ♦ A 7 5
                    ♣ A Q
```

Observe that a club lead defeats the hand, whereas the spade opening enables West to fulfill the slam.

6. *Pass.* Surely you should be delighted to defeat six hearts and score your honors in the bargain. To double would be an example of pure greed. It is true that you must defeat the heart slam, but you have no defense against six or seven no trump for that matter. When this hand was actually played, South doubled vehemently. West analyzed the situation correctly and bid six no trump. He was able to bring home the slam with an overtrick.

7. *Two Spades.* The customary procedure for showing a six-four distribution is to rebid the six-card suit first and then showing your four-card suit, if convenient. Since your spade suit is so much stronger than your heart holding, there is no reason to depart from this policy. To rebid two hearts would temporarily give partner the impression that you had either four or five spades together with four hearts rather than the actual six-four holding.

8. *Double.* The opposition has struggled to reach a game, and by the distribution of your cards, you know that no suits will break favorably for them. You have the spades and diamonds bottled up, and partner probably has hearts well covered. Moreover, you have a good suit that can be set up in one or two leads, and the resulting mayhem may add up to 500 or 700 points. Oddly enough, if you were sitting in the North position, your cards would be lying favorably for the East-West pair, and a double would be foolhardy. Be quick to double for penalties when the location of your cards can be expected to give declarer a rough time.

9. *Pass.* Your partner has made a game forcing bid, and while you would have cheerfully proceeded to four hearts, the overcall by East should not pass by unheeded. Partner may welcome an opportunity to double for penalties. If he should do so, it would not be distasteful to you. Partner's hand:

♠ Q J 10 9   ♥ J 10 7 6   ♦ A Q   ♣ K 9 4

10. *Pass.* The double of two no trump is strictly for penalties, and partner is not interested in your hand whatsoever. No doubt he has a long diamond suit which can be set up immediately together with two or more key cards which will afford him entry. To bid three spades because you are "busted" is a severe breach of partnership.

1. As South you hold:

         ♠ A K 6 4 3 2   ♥ A Q 4   ♦ K 3   ♣ 3 2

The bidding has proceeded:

SOUTH	NORTH
1 ♠	2 ♠
?	

2. East-West vulnerable. As South you hold:

         ♠ 3   ♥ 10 9 8 7 6 2   ♦ 4 3 2   ♣ A K 2

The bidding has proceeded:

WEST	NORTH	EAST	SOUTH
1 ♠	3 ♥	4 ♥	?
	(pre-emptive)		

3. As South you hold:

         ♠ 3 2   ♥ 8 5   ♦ K Q J 8 7 6 2   ♣ 6 5

The bidding has proceeded:

NORTH	SOUTH
1 NT	?

4. As South you hold:

         ♠ 7 6 3   ♥ A K Q 9 4 2   ♦ 4 2   ♣ 8 7

The bidding has proceeded:

NORTH	SOUTH
1 ♦	1 ♥
1 NT	?

Quiz 4

5. As South you hold:

♠ 10 2   ♥ K 5   ♦ A 7 3 2   ♣ 9 8 7 6 5

The bidding has proceeded:

NORTH	SOUTH
1 NT	?

6. You hold, as South:

♠ 3 2   ♥ 6 4   ♦ A 10 7 2   ♣ K 9 8 7 6

The bidding has proceeded:

NORTH	SOUTH
1 NT	?

7. East-West vulnerable. As South you hold:

♠ A J   ♥ J 10 3   ♦ Q 9 7 5   ♣ Q 8 6 4

The bidding has proceeded:

SOUTH	WEST	NORTH	EAST
Pass	Pass	1 ♥	2 ♦
2 ♥	Pass	Pass	3 ♦
?			

8. As South you hold:

♠ K 3   ♥ J 10 9   ♦ K Q 7 6 5 2   ♣ K 6

The bidding has proceeded:

SOUTH	WEST	NORTH	EAST
Pass	Pass	1 ♦	Pass
?			

9. North-South vulnerable. As South you hold:

♠ A K 10 9 4   ♥ A K 5   ♦ 4   ♣ 10 9 6 2

The bidding has proceeded:

EAST	SOUTH	WEST	NORTH
1 ♣	Double	2 ♣	Pass
Pass	2 ♠	3 ♣	3 ♠
Pass	?		

10. As South you hold:

♠ A 6 3   ♥ 7 5 2   ♦ K J 10 9 4   ♣ Q 10

The bidding has proceeded:

NORTH	EAST	SOUTH	WEST
1 ♣	Pass	1 ♦	1 ♠
3 ♦	Pass	?	

Quiz 4 – ANSWERS

1. *Four Spades.* Our policy is to bid a game without further ado when we see it. Since our hand re-evaluates to 20 points after partner's raise, and he has at most 10, prospects of a slam are quite remote. We favor the direct approach to the game, leaving the enemy to guess what to lead. It might be argued that three clubs is a good tactical maneuver which may steer West off the most advantageous lead. This may be true, but remember partner is not barred from raising to four clubs — a call which may permit East to double for purposes of obtaining a lead in that suit. All in all, it pays to remain mum and leave the adversaries in the dark.

2. *Five Clubs.* You have an excellent sacrifice against five spades and should take steps to direct the defense if the opposition persists to a slam in that suit. Your bid of five clubs prepares the way. You are certainly willing to compete up to six hearts with this favorable vulnerability, and your call in clubs will make the enemy give up the ghost. It is true that the opposition will be defeated in six spades, but partner will be on lead, and failure to come out with a club could result in losing the hand. Your five-club call dismisses that possibility.

3. *Three No Trump.* Since you have no way of finding out whether you can make one, two, or three no trump, we suggest you bid a game with dispatch and leave the opposition to guess the best defense. If partner holds the ace of diamonds among his assets and can obtain the lead in time, your game contract has an excellent chance for success.

4. *Three No Trump.* Your good heart suit will take tricks in no trump as well as in hearts, and even though your hand has but nine high-card points, the value of the fifth and sixth hearts cannot be overlooked. A call of three hearts does not receive our warm approval, for partner might feel obliged to raise to four and you might lose the hand on the adverse opening lead through partner's holdings. A contract of three no trump, on the other hand, appears to have an excellent chance for success.

5. *Pass.* While you have seven high-card points and a five-card suit, your high cards are not with your long suit, which places partner with the burden of producing the matching high cards to eventually promote the long cards in that suit into winners. Since partner can have at most 18 points, we do not feel optimistic about the hand.

6. This hand differs from the previous hand in that our high cards are concentrated in our long suits, and we feel that our hand will supply enough playing strength opposite a maximum no-trump opening to produce a game. We therefore bid two no trump.

7. *Double.* Since you have previously limited your hand by a pass and a mere raise in partner's suit, you are perfectly justified in taking some aggressive action. Partner is not bound by your call and may bid three hearts if he finds a three-diamond doubled contract unattractive. On the other hand, if he chooses to pass, the set might be rewarding.

8. *Three No Trump.* This is one of the rare instances where a passed hand is justified in leaping to game. Your six-card match in partner's suit has given your hand tremendous playing value, and a game at no trump should have an excellent play. While you have 13 points and a six-card suit, we do not recommend opening this hand. It lacks defensive strength, and since you have an optional opening bid at best, you are better off passing.

9. *Four Spades.* While partner has not guaranteed a maximum raise for his bid, he is more or less marked with at most one club on the auction, and all he needs to produce a game is length in trumps and a key queen. When you feel your chances for making a game are good, don't worry about your possible lack of points—bid it.

10. *Three Spades.* This bid serves a dual purpose. It will enable partner to bid three no trump if that is the best contract, or he can look around for a slam if his hand is suited for the purpose. Partner has opened the bidding and jumped; your hand is almost as good as an opening bid, since the queen of clubs has been promoted by virtue of partner's bidding that suit. There is the possibility of a slam.

1. You hold as South:

♠ Q J 6 3   ♥ 4 3 2   ♦ 7 5 3 2   ♣ J 3

The bidding has proceeded:

NORTH	EAST	SOUTH	WEST
1 ♣	Pass	Pass	Double
2 ♠	Pass	?	

2. As South you hold:

♠ K 9 7 5   ♥ A 4 2   ♦ A 10 7 6 3   ♣ 3

The bidding has proceeded:

WEST	NORTH	EAST	SOUTH
Pass	Pass	1 ♣	Double
Redouble	2 ♠	Pass	?

3. With East-West vulnerable, as South you hold:

♠ A K 7 5 3   ♥ 10 8   ♦ J 9 5 3   ♣ 3 2

The bidding has proceeded:

NORTH	EAST	SOUTH	WEST
1 ♣	Pass	1 ♠	Pass
2 ♣	Pass	Pass	2 ♦
Pass	Pass	?	

4. North-South are vulnerable. You as South hold:

♠ A Q J 9 5   ♥ 6 4 3   ♦ A Q J 2   ♣ K

The bidding has proceeded:

SOUTH	WEST	NORTH	EAST
1 ♠	2 ♥	3 ♣	3 ♥
4 ♦	4 ♥	6 ♠	Pass
Pass	7 ♥	Pass	Pass
?			

5. As South you hold:

♠ Q 7 5 3   ♥ Q 2   ♦ 7 6 4 3   ♣ 4 3 2

The bidding has proceeded:

NORTH	EAST	SOUTH	WEST
1 ♠	Pass	Pass	2 ♣
3 ♥	Pass	?	

6. As South you hold:

♠ Q J 10 9   ♥ J 10 9 8   ♦ 3   ♣ A 9 7 6

The bidding has proceeded:

NORTH	EAST	SOUTH	WEST
Pass	1 ♠	Pass	2 ♣
2 NT	Double	?	

7. As South you hold:

♠ A 7 6   ♥ A 5 3   ♦ Q 9 5   ♣ K J 10 2

The bidding has proceeded:

NORTH	EAST	SOUTH	WEST
1 ♦	Pass	2 NT	Pass
3 ♣	Pass	?	

8. As South you hold:

    ♠ 3   ♥ A 7 6 3   ♦ Q J 9 3   ♣ K 10 9 3

The bidding has proceeded:

NORTH	EAST	SOUTH	WEST
1 ♣	Pass	1 ♦	1 ♥
3 ♣	Pass	?	

9. As South you hold:

    ♠ A Q 4   ♥ A K 7   ♦ A 3 2   ♣ 9 4 3 2

The bidding has proceeded:

SOUTH	WEST	NORTH	EAST
1 NT	Pass	2 ♣	2 ♦
?			

10. As South you hold:

    ♠ J 3   ♥ 10 7 5   ♦ A   ♣ A K Q J 6 4 2

The bidding has proceeded:

SOUTH	WEST	NORTH	EAST
1 ♣	1 ♠	Double	Pass
?			

Quiz **5**–ANSWERS

1. *Three Spades.* Partner has shown a decided interest in game despite your warning pass on the first round. Since your spade and club holdings have been promoted by virtue of his bids in these suits, you should feel inclined to enthusiasm and show this by offering him a raise in spades. In light of the fact that you were willing to play the hand at one club, partner cannot expect too much in the way of strength from you.

2. *Three Spades.* If you have a timid partner, four spades is a worthwhile call. You have 15 points in support of partner's suit, and partner should have at least an average hand. A game call, therefore, should not be out of reach.

3.   *Double.*   Such a call is purely co-operative, and partner need not stand for it if his hand is unsuited for such an action. The facts are all before him. You have indicated a none too robust hand with a tolerance for clubs when you passed his minimum rebid. If he decides to stand for the double, you may well defeat the contract two or three tricks. If the cards lie unfortunately for your side, two diamonds doubled won't yield a game to the opposition. All in all, you have a lot going for you by making a penalty double at this point.

4.   *Seven Spades.*   Partner has indicated that he holds first-round control of hearts by his failure to double the seven-heart call for penalties. Since he appears to be interested in the prospects for a grand slam, you should be quick to bid it. Your king of clubs has taken on an added luster since partner bid that suit at the level of three, and there is no reason why the grand slam should not be a laydown.

5.   *Four Spades.*   You have full values for your jump, since you have already passed one spade, and should bid game in spades with alacrity. A bid of three spades would leave partner in the dark, since he would not be certain whether you were enthusiastic in your choice or were merely taking a preference.

6.   *Four Hearts.*   This is a tactical maneuver intended to catapult the opposition to a high level. If they choose to compete further you have a nice surprise for them and can double for penalties. If they elect instead to double your contract for penalties, you will either come close to making your contract or be defeated by at most one trick. Partner has shown a mediocre two-suited hand by virtue of his employment of the unusual no-trump overcall in this position. His holding:

♠ None   ♥ Q 7 6 5 4 3   ♦ A J 10 5 4   ♣ 4 3

7.   *Three Spades or Three Hearts.*   Partner has shown an unbalanced holding, and your controls together with your splendid fit in clubs should make a slam effort attractive. Your cue bid of three hearts or three spades, followed by a raise in clubs, will alert partner as to the nature of your message. Since you failed to respond with a major suit at the level of one, he will take your subsequent call at the three level as a slam try and can then act accordingly.

8. *Three Hearts—and await partner's next move.* Your hand has become more impressive since partner bid three clubs. After partner has opened and jumped, it behooves you to become mildly slam-conscious, and your cue bid attests to that fact.

9. *Pass.* Partner may be able to show a five-card major suit or possibly double for penalties. Either bid will be suitable to us. Should he elect to pass, it would indicate that he had very little values for the employment of the Two Club Convention. His hand:

♠ K 9 6 5   ♥ Q J 9 5 3   ♦ 5   ♣ Q 10 8

10. *Three No Trump.* While it is quite possible that one spade will be defeated, you have a hand which figures to score offensively, and a call of three no trump is recommended. This does not bar partner from proceeding. If he is inclined to carry on, then there is a good chance that a slam in clubs is within reach.

1. As South you hold:

♠ A J 3 ♥ A K Q 9 5 ♦ A 3 ♣ A 10 5

The bidding has proceeded:

SOUTH	NORTH
2 NT	4 ♠
?	

What do you bid now?

2. East-West vulnerable — as South you hold:

♠ J 10 9 4 ♥ K 2 ♦ A 3 2 ♣ 9 7 6 5

The bidding has proceeded:

NORTH	EAST	SOUTH	WEST
3 ♥	Pass	?	

What do you bid now?

3. As South you hold:

♠ 6 4 3 ♥ A K Q 10 4 ♦ A K Q 2 ♣ 6

The bidding has proceeded:

SOUTH	WEST	NORTH	EAST
1 ♥	1 ♠	1 NT	Pass
?			

What do you bid now?

4. As South you hold:

♠ J 10   ♥ K   ♦ A K J 10 5   ♣ A K Q J 10

The bidding has proceeded:

SOUTH	WEST	NORTH	EAST
1 ♦	Pass	Pass	1 ♥
3 ♣	Pass	4 ♦	Pass
?			

What do you bid now?

5. As South you hold:

♠ A K 9 7   ♥ 7 4   ♦ K 10 9 4   ♣ K 6 3

The bidding has proceeded:

SOUTH	NORTH
1 ♦	1 ♠
2 ♠	3 ♠
?	

What do you bid?

6. As South you hold:

♠ Q 7 5   ♥ A 10 9 4   ♦ 10 9 3 2   ♣ K 2

The bidding has proceeded:

NORTH	EAST	SOUTH	WEST
1 ♠	Pass	2 ♠	Pass
Pass	Double	?	

What do you bid?

7. As South you hold:

♠ A   ♥ 10 9 7 5 2   ♦ J 9 7   ♣ 9 8 4 3

The bidding has proceeded:

WEST	NORTH	EAST	SOUTH
1 ♠	Pass	2 ♥	Pass
3 ♥	Pass	4 ♠	Pass
4 NT	Pass	5 ♦	Pass
6 ♠	Pass	Pass	?

What do you bid?

8. As South you hold:

♠ Q 7 5   ♥ K 10 6 4   ♦ 7 6 3   ♣ 4 3 2

The bidding has proceeded:

WEST	NORTH	EAST	SOUTH
1 NT	Double	Pass	?

9. As South you hold:

♠ 10 9 6 4   ♥ A Q 6 5   ♦ 3   ♣ 9 4 3 2

The bidding has proceeded:

NORTH	EAST	SOUTH
1 ♠	Double	?

10. As South you hold:

♠ A Q J 10 4 3 2   ♥ None   ♦ K Q 2   ♣ K 7 3

The bidding has proceeded:

SOUTH	WEST	NORTH	EAST
1 ♠	2 ♥	3 ♦	4 ♥
4 ♠	5 ♥	Pass	Pass
6 ♦	6 ♥	Pass	Pass
?			

What do you bid?

Quiz 6—ANSWERS

1. *Six Spades.* Partner can be relied upon to hold a six-card suit headed by the king-queen or a seven-card suit to the king or queen. In either case, a slam in spades has an excellent chance for success. Remember, a bid of three spades after a two no-trump opening is forcing for one round. It follows that a jump to game would show an impressive suit. Your wealth of controls together with a splendid side suit should make a slam effort odds-on.

2. *Four Hearts.* If the adverse cards are divided, you might well steal the hand with this bid, for both of your opponents may credit each other with a sorry holding. To pass three hearts leaves the door open for enemy competition which will yield an almost certain game for them.

3. *Three Diamonds.* Partner has bid freely and can be expected to hold a hand of about average strength. It behooves you to insist upon game, and your three-diamond call is a step in that direction. If partner returns to three hearts, you will, of course, proceed to game in that suit. If he rebids three no trump, that contract should not prove to be distasteful, since he has been forewarned about the club suit. If he carries on to four diamonds, you can try four hearts, which will give him a choice of contracts.

4. *Five Diamonds.* We agree that a slam may be on hand if partner has five diamonds and the ace of spades, but remember, partner passed one diamond, and the likelihood that he holds such a hand is rather remote. Five diamonds, on the other hand should not be a bad gamble, since one can always pray for a singleton spade in partner's hand or a situation where the opposition fails to cash three quick tricks promptly, which will permit us to discard on our good club suit.

5. *Four Spades.* It might be argued that the South hand holds but 14 points in support and therefore is a minimum holding for the initial raise. It is true that the point count is the least the law allows, but the nature of the South hand cannot be disregarded. It is made up of an ace and three kings, and these cards are mildly disregarded in comparison by the 4–3–2–1 point count. If the hand held 14 points composed of queens and jacks, we would, quite naturally, be disposed to pass.

6. *Redouble.* You have maximum values for your raise and also a hand that will score defensively. The redouble sends this message to partner, and he may be able to double an adverse club contract. You are quite prepared to take care of the red suits. It would be improper to bid three spades or to pass. If you chose to pass, and your right-hand opponent called in clubs, your proper subsequent action would become a question mark.

7. *Double.* This calls for the lead of dummy's first bid suit, which is hearts. Since East has bid the suit at the level of two and West has raised, partner can be expected to hold at most a singleton. You, of course, expect to obtain the lead with the ace of trumps and give him a ruff. It may be argued that the defense might bid six no trump and make it. This is quite possible, but remember, you expect them to make six spades unless partner makes a specific lead. The mathematics are as follows: assuming that without a heart lead the opposition will make their slam, and a double, which calls for a heart lead,

will defeat the slam, your gain is 980 plus 100 points for the doubled undertrick or 1080 points. On the other hand if they make the hand despite your double, they will score 1210 points (the value of a doubled non-vulnerable slam in spades). However, you think that they will make the slam *unless* partner leads a heart. Therefore your potential gain is 1080 and your potential loss is 1210 — 980 or 230 points. In a nutshell you have odds of over four to one in favor of the double.

8. *Pass.* The double of one no trump is intended for penalties and should not be taken out unless doubler's partner is trickless and has a long suit. You have 5 points in high cards, and partner should have the equal of a one no-trump opening himself. At the beginning you outpoint the opposition by at least 21 to 19. Also, your partner's cards are strategically located behind the no-trumper, and the set may prove to be substantial.

9. *Three Spades.* You have a hand which is worth nine points in support of spades and should take this opportunity to show your wares. A redouble would indicate a hand that is average in strength, and your hand is worth but 6 points in high-card strength. Also, your length in spades might devalue partner's potential defensive strength in that suit. All in all, the jump to three spades gives partner the better picture of your values.

10. *Six Spades.* When there is a reasonable doubt as to whether your side can defeat the enemy in a contract which has been reached by highly competitive bidding, you should bid once more in preference to running the risk that their contract is iron-clad. The mathematics of the situation are as follows: if the opposition is left unmolested and make their six-heart contract, it will cost in the neighborhood of 1000 points. If, at the conclusion of the hand, it is discovered that your partnership could have made six spades, the net swing will be approximately 2000 points. On the other hand, if you could have defeated them as many as two tricks and instead are doubled in six spades and are off two, your negative result will be a total of 600 points. We are quite prepared to pay off 600 points but will not concede 2000 points in such a close decision. The moral of such a venture is—when in doubt, bid once more.

1. As South you hold:

♠ 3   ♥ A K Q 5 4 3 2   ♦ 7 5   ♣ 9 7 3

The bidding has proceeded:

NORTH	SOUTH
1 ♣	?

What do you bid?

2. As South you hold:

♠ A   ♥ A 6 5 3 2   ♦ K 6 4 3   ♣ Q 10 8

The bidding has proceeded:

EAST	SOUTH	WEST	NORTH
1 ♣	1 ♥	Pass	1 NT
Pass	?		

What do you bid?

3. Both sides are vulnerable. As South you hold:

♠ A Q 3 2   ♥ None   ♦ A 10 7 5 3   ♣ K 7 4 2

The bidding has proceeded:

EAST	SOUTH	WEST	NORTH
1 ♦	Pass	Pass	1 ♥
Pass	1 NT	Pass	2 ♥
Pass	?		

What do you bid?

4. As South you hold:

♠ 6   ♥ A J 10 9 5   ♦ K 9 4   ♣ A K Q 3

The bidding has proceeded:

SOUTH	WEST	NORTH	EAST
1 ♥	1 ♠	Pass	2 ♠
?			

What do you bid?

5. As South you hold:

♠ K Q 4 2   ♥ Q 9 7 5   ♦ A 7 6 3   ♣ A

The bidding has proceeded:

NORTH	SOUTH
1 NT	2 ♣
2 ♠	?

What do you bid?

6. As South you hold:

♠ A K 6 4   ♥ None   ♦ A K 6 3   ♣ A 7 4 3 2

The bidding has proceeded:

NORTH	EAST	SOUTH
3 ♥	Pass	?

What do you bid?

7. As South you hold:

♠ Q J 7 6 2   ♥ 4 3   ♦ K 9 5   ♣ A J 3

The bidding has proceeded:

NORTH	SOUTH
1 ♠	?

What do you bid?

8. North-South vulnerable. As South you hold:

    ♠ A Q 3 2   ♥ K Q 7 5   ♦ 10 8 4   ♣ A 3

    The bidding has proceeded:

WEST	NORTH	EAST	SOUTH
3 ♦	3 ♥	5 ♦	?

    What do you bid?

9. As South you hold:

    ♠ 10 7 3   ♥ A Q 6 2   ♦ K 4 3   ♣ 7 6 2

    The bidding has proceeded:

NORTH	SOUTH
1 ♠	1 NT
2 ♥	?

10. You are South. East opens with 1 ♣. You hold:

    ♠ 3   ♥ A Q 8 6 4   ♦ A K J 5   ♣ 8 3 2

    The bidding has proceeded:

EAST	SOUTH
1 ♣	?

    What do you bid?

Quiz 7 – ANSWERS

1. *Four Hearts.* We do concede that this may turn out badly in a case where you have caused a slam to be missed, but it is to be pointed out that your action does not absolutely bar partner from further participation, and if we do miss a slam we will have our apology ready for partner. Rather than offer the opposition a chance to find their fit, the recommended action of four hearts will usually produce the best result.

2. *Pass.* While it appears that the hand will play better in a suit contract, a little reflection will convince you that a pass is the best action on the hand in question. Since partner has shown no interest in the spade suit, the enemy should have a minimum

of eight cards between them in that suit. If you bid two diamonds, and partner passes, the opener may take liberties and probe for a spade contract at this convenient level. It is better to play the hand in the possibly inferior contract of one no trump rather than run the risk of losing the contract altogether.

3. *Pass.* When signs of a decided misfit are eminent, any un-doubled contract is considered to be a safe haven. Any attempt to improve the contract at this point might alert the opposition enough to double the final contract for penalties.

4. *Double.* You have an excellent hand, and there is no reason to insist on a club or heart contract by bidding three clubs. On the bidding, partner has a rather poor hand, but he may have five or six diamonds, in which case three diamonds might be the best contract. If by chance partner passes your takeout double for penalties, the subsequent set will be suited to your taste.

5. *Six Spades.* Since there is no absolute way to determine whether you can make six or seven, we suggest you bid the slam forthwith and leave the opposition to finding the best defense. To probe for grand slam possibilities by bidding three clubs or three diamonds might give away vital informa-tion to the enemy, and they may find a particular lead which could beat the slam. Moreover, your hand in support of spades is valued at 18 points, and since partner cannot hold more than 18 himself, your total assets do not reach grand-slam proportions.

6. *Four Hearts.* It may appear heroic to raise partner with a void in his trump suit, but actually it is the only reasonable call. A bid of three no trump could prove disastrous unless partner has fillers in clubs—and his pre-emptive opening has promised only good hearts. For those players with optimistic tendencies, we look upon a slam contract as a poor gamble despite the five honor tricks held by South. A non-vulnerable pre-emptive bid will seldom contain seven sure winners as well as a solid trump suit which are the ingredients required by partner to make a slam effort plausible. Your five honor tricks should be able to swing the game in his suit. His hand:

♠ 3   ♥ K Q J 10 9 3 2   ♦ 8 7 5   ♣ 8 6

7. *Two Clubs.* There is no satisfactory response with this hand. It is too good for two spades and not good enough for three spades, which promises game. Nor is it the proper type for a jump to four. The best bet is to make a temporary bid of two clubs, intending to give a spade raise on the next round.

8. *Six Hearts.* Partner appears to have at most one diamond, and we trust that the slam effort will be reasonable. This is only a side issue on this hand, however, for the enemy will surely prefer to take the non-vulnerable sacrifice of seven diamonds rather than take the chance on beating our slam.

9. *Three Hearts.* Partner's hand is not limited to a minimum opening bid, and the added knowledge of a secondary fit together with a maximum one no-trump response might tip the scales in a gameward direction. Two spades is a cautious approach, enabling partner to continue if he has extra values. We feel that a pass is rather a timid call with your splendid values.

10. *One Heart.* While you have the high-card strength to justify a double, such a procedure is not advisable since partner will probably respond with one spade, which will make it necessary to bid two hearts. Since your suit is rather shaky, such a bid might be severely punished.